REFLECTIONS ON
THE FAILURE OF SOCIALISM

OTHER BOOKS BY MAX EASTMAN

Enjoyment of Poetry
Journalism Versus Art
Understanding Germany
The Sense of Humor
Since Lenin Died
Leon Trotsky, the Portrait of a Youth
Marx and Lenin, the Science of Revolution
Venture, a novel
The Literary Mind, Its Place in an Age of Science
Artists in Uniform
Art and the Life of Action
Enjoyment of Laughter
The End of Socialism in Russia
Stalin's Russia and the Crisis in Socialism
Marxism Is It Science
Heroes I Have Known
Enjoyment of Living
The Road to Abundance (*with Jacob Rosin*)

POETRY

Child of the Amazons and Other Poems
Colors of Life
Kinds of Love
Lot's Wife, a dramatic poem
Poems of Five Decades

TRANSLATIONS

The Real Situation in Russia by Leon Trotsky
Gabriel by Pushkin
A History of the Russian Revolution by Leon Trotsky
The Revolution Betrayed by Leon Trotsky

EDITED

Capital and Other Writings by Karl Marx
Anthology for the Enjoyment of Poetry

MAX EASTMAN

Reflections

on

the

FAILURE

of

SOCIALISM

THE DEVIN-ADAIR COMPANY
NEW YORK
1955

Book designed by Lewis F. White
Printed in the United States of America
Library of Congress Catalog Card Number: 55–7352

14491

CONTENTS

Biographical Introduction

PEOPLE who read these reflections may wonder how I arrived at the understanding that socialism has failed. I am describing the whole experience in another book, but here a brief glance at the intellectual road I traveled may be helpful. It has not been so winding a road as some may think.

I stated the aim of my political activities in two articles in the *Masses* in 1916: not to reform men, or even primarily reform the world, but to "make all men as free to live and realize the world as it is possible for them to be." In this the years have brought no change.

In those same articles I dismissed Marx's philosophic system, his idea that socialism is historically necessary, as "a rationalization of his wish," and declared: "We must alter and remodel what he wrote, and make of it and of what else our recent science offers, a doctrine that shall clearly have the nature of hypothesis."

7

The hypothesis, as I conceived it, was that by intensifying the working class struggle, and pursuing it to victory either at the polls or in a revolution, we could "socialize the means of production," and thus extend democracy from politics into economics. That, I thought, would give every man a chance to build a life in his own chosen way. It would "liberate the proletariat and therewith all society," to use a Marxian formula that I liked to quote.

To me, in short, socialism was not a philosophy of history, or of life—much less a religion—but a large-scale social-scientific experiment. I came to it by a process of thought rather than feeling. I had no personal envies or resentments; I was happily circumstanced and wisely brought up; I thought of myself as free. I wanted to extend that freedom to all men; I wanted to see a society without distinctions of caste, class, race, money-power—without exploitation, without the "wage system." I knew this could not be brought about by preaching; I had observed the effects of preaching. I was captivated by the idea that it might be brought about by self-interested struggle on the part of those most deprived under the present system. Thus *the class struggle as a method* was the very center of my socialist belief. The articles quoted above were entitled "Towards Liberty, The Method of Progress," and they were meant to be the first chapters of a book.

It was juvenile of me to imagine that humanity as a whole, especially by splitting itself into two halves, could turn a whole period of history into a scientific experiment. Science requires a scientist, or at least an engineer, and the engineer in this case would have to have dictatorial power. But that thought, if it entered my mind, I managed to elude. I worked out a socialism of my own which enabled me to take an independent position on many concrete questions: feminism, population-control, peace and war. Both the doctrine of class morals and the propaganda of class hate I rejected. I could think freely on such questions because my socialism was not a mystical cure-all, but merely a plan which I considered practical for solving the one specific problem of making freedom more general and democracy more democratic.

Although I was a member of the Socialist Party, the magazines I edited from 1912 to 1922, the *Masses* and the *Liberator,* were arrantly independent, and I was pretty regularly flayed alive by the party officials for some heresy or other. It was usually a revolutionary heresy. I was decidedly at the red end of the party spectrum. Still it wasn't always the reformists as against the revolutionists that I attacked. As often it was the dogmatism of both. Naturally in my attempt to make Marxism over into an experimental science, I waged a continual war on the bigotry, the cant, the know-it-allism, of the party priesthood. This I think distinguished the policy of the old *Masses** and the *Liberator* as much as their militant insistence on the class struggle. I was always close friends with the I.W.W., and on good terms even with the anarchists, although I lectured them on their childish innocence of the concept of method. I was not afraid, either, of the word liberal with a small *l,* although I had my own definition of it. "A liberal mind," I wrote in the *Masses* for September 1917, "is a mind that is able to imagine itself believing anything. It is the only mind that is capable of judging beliefs, or that can hold strongly without bigotry to a belief of its own."

When the Bolsheviks seized power in Russia in October 1917, shocking the whole world of progressive and even moderate socialist opinion, I backed them to the limit in the

* I use the word "old" to distinguish the *Masses* from the *New Masses,* a magazine founded years later by a totally different group of people, and which, under the control of the Communist party, developed a policy contrary in almost every detail to what the *Masses* and the *Liberator* stood for. I have discussed this more fully in *Enjoyment of Living,* p. 415.

Liberator. I raised the money to send John Reed to Russia, and published his articles that grew into the famous book, *Ten Days That Shook the World.* I was about the only "red" still out of jail in those violent days, and my magazine was for a time the sole source of unbewildered information about what was happening in Russia. Its circulation reached a peak of sixty thousand.

When Lenin's pamphlet called in English "The Soviets at Work" was published—the same that won Whittaker Chambers to communism—I was enraptured. The monumental practicality, the resolute factualness, of Lenin's mind, combined as almost never before with a glowing regard for poor and oppressed people, anxiety over their freedom, devotion to the idea of their entrance into power, swept me off my feet. I still think it one of the noblest—and now saddest—of political documents. It convinced me that Lenin's mind was experimental. In every line he seemed to realize my ideal of a scientific revolutionist. I greeted him in two articles in the *Liberator* as "a Statesman of a New Order," and dedicated myself with no doctrinal reservations to the defense of his principles of action and his Soviet regime.

Attacking those who accused him of dogmatism, I exclaimed: "I have never seen a sign in any speech or writing of Lenin that he regarded the Marxian theory as anything more than a scientific hypothesis in process of verification."

There were few translations from Russian in those days. I had to go to Russia and learn the language before I found out that Lenin was a true believer in the Marxian mystique. He was, to be sure, more high-handed with its postulates than any other believer—much more so than Trotsky. He had the trick, as Karl Radek once remarked to me, of "deciding a question on the basis of the facts and then fixing it up with the theory afterward." He also had Hegel's notion of "dialectic logic" to help him with this trick. I did not know enough then to distinguish between the limited freedom dispensed to the faithful by this ingenious notion, and the complete freedom of a mind dealing only with facts, purposes, and plans of action. I gave my heart to Lenin more completely than I have to any other leader, and fought for the Bolsheviks on the battlefield of American opinion with all the influence my voice and magazine possessed. From the October revolution until Baron Wrangel was swept out of the Crimea, I was engaged in a civil war, and my socialist convictions grew hard and firm. It took a long time after that, a steady and merciless bombardment of hostile and unanswerable facts, to unsettle them.

Still I was far enough from fanatical when I sailed for Russia in 1922 to remark to my friends that I was "going over to find out whether what I have been saying is true." I arrived in September, in time to learn a little Russian before I attended the fourth congress of the Third International. I was not a delegate and had no official status, but the *Liberator* was well enough known so that I was hospitably received as a guest. Later on, Trotsky, who consented to cooperate with me on a biographical portrait, gave me a portentous document bearing his signature and the seal of the Red Army, asking everybody in Russia to receive me cordially and attend to my needs. I traveled wherever I wanted to with that document, and saw whatever I asked to see.

I traveled at the height of the swift recovery that followed the adoption of the New Economic Policy, and I experienced Soviet life at its best. Although surprised and shocked by some features of the experiment, I found ground for great hope also. Only one thing seemed to me calamitously bad. That was the bigotry and Byzantine scholasticism which had grown up around the sacred scriptures of Marxism. Hegel, Marx, Engels, Plekhanov, Lenin—these men's books contained for the Bolsheviks the last word of human knowledge. They were not science, they were revelation. Nothing remained for living thinkers to do but apply them, gloss them, dispute about them, expatiate on them, find in them the germs of every new thought or thing that came into the world. Instead of liberating the mind of man, the Bolshevik Revolution locked it into a state's prison tighter than ever before. No flight of thought was conceivable, no poetic promenade even, no sneak through the doors or peep out of a window in this pre-Darwinian dungeon called Dialectic Materialism. No one in the western world has any idea of the degree to which Soviet minds are closed and sealed tight against any idea but the premises and conclusions of this antique system of wishful thinking. So far as concerns the advance of human understanding, the Soviet Union is a gigantic roadblock, armed, fortified, and defended by indoctrinated automatons made out of flesh, blood, and brains in the robot-factories they call schools.

I felt this barbarous thing more keenly than any other disappointment in the land of my dreams. I was sure it contained the seeds of priest rule and police rule. Any state religion, as all the great liberals have pointed out, is death to human freedom. The separation of church and state is one of the main measures of protection against tyranny. But the Marxian religion makes this separation impossible, for its *creed* is politics; its church *is* the state. There is no hope within its dogmas of any evolution toward the free society it promises.

For these reasons, instead of writing the travel stories expected of me about "Life under the Soviets," I went into the reading room of the Marx-Engels Institute in Moscow and got down to work on my old unfinished partial torso of a book, "Towards Liberty, the Method of Progress." Although not deceived that anybody would pay prompt attention to me, I thought it my duty to the revolution to attack this road-block, this prodigy of obtuseness parading as ultimate wisdom, in the only way it could be attacked, by an unanswerable demonstration of the conflict between Marxism and scientific method.

I stayed a year and nine months in Russia, and put in a major part of my time learning Russian and reading, mostly in that language, the essential literature on which the actions of the Bolsheviks were based. Leaving Russia in June 1924, I spent the next three years in western Europe, where I finished a book on the subject and named it *Marx and Lenin, the Science of Revolution.* It was published in London in 1926. The Anglo-Saxon world had so little interest then in Marxian theory that I had to advance the money for its publication. But Albert and Charles Boni bought sheets and published it a year later in New York. *La Nouvelle Revue Française* published a French translation the following year. My money investment was well repaid. But my success in undermining the roadblock in Russia was not conspicuous. The copy I sent to the Marx-Engels Institute was returned by the Post Office marked: "Denied admission by the Department of Publications." The only murmur to come out of Russia was from the great scientist, Ivan Pavlov, who surprised me with a letter in his own hand sent fearlessly through the mail: "I endorse completely your criticism of the philosophical foundation of Marxism." And he added this contribution to my painfully slow recovery from socialism: "There isn't any science of revolution, and there won't be for a long time. There is only a groping of the life force, partly guided empirically, of those who have a much-embracing and strong common sense. Our Bolshevik Revolution, with its details so disastrous to our intellectual and moral development, I consider an anachronism which (of this I am convinced) will repeat itself in this form never and nowhere in the civilized world. Such is my deepest understanding of these matters."

In that book I wrote as a believer in the Soviet system, and I still imputed to Lenin a stride forward, however unconscious, toward the attitude of experimental science, calling him by contrast with his more orthodox opponents an "engineer of revolution." There was a great deal of truth in this, but I still managed to elude its implications. I thought it was a wonderful and hopeful thing that Lenin had succeeded, by basing himself on the Marxian analysis of class forces, in throwing a net over the whole of Russian society, and gathering the power into his hands and that of a party dedicated to building socialism.

This theoretic conception stood firm in my mind, even though I had seen before leaving Russia what I now believe to be its direct and normal consequence: the usurpation of power by a tyrant having no honest instinct for the liberties of men. I had not only seen, but very carefully studied the plot by which Stalin made himself master after Lenin's death. Besides studying his maneuvers, I attended the party congress of May 1924, at which his open attack was launched and Trotsky's prestige in the party destroyed. Behind the scenes at that congress Trotsky told me in whispers the drift and essential details of the suppressed document called "Lenin's Testament." I was leaving Russia in a few days, and I spent those days gathering, with his encouragement, what further documents I needed to expose the plot and explain it. To do this I laid aside my work on Marxism, and wrote the little book called *Since Lenin Died*, which remains, I think, an authentic source for the history of the conflict about leadership which followed Lenin's death.

In the evolution of my socialist opinions that book marked a rather modest step. My conclusion was only a caution to revolutionists in other countries against accepting in the name of Leninism "the international authority of a group against whom Lenin's dying words were a warning, and who have preserved that authority by suppressing the essential texts of Lenin." Fourteen years would pass before I was able to see in that group, not only an *enemy* of Lenin's plans, but a *result* of the revolution as conceived and engineered by him.

I had said enough in my two books, however, to ostracize me completely from the official communist movement. When I came home from Europe in 1927 most of my old political friends refused to speak to me on the street. I was a traitor, a renegade, a pariah, a veritable untouchable, so far as the communists were concerned. And as the bitterness mounted, this mood spread to the radical, and even in some degree to the liberal, intelligentsia as a whole. To get rid of my facts, I was of course promptly and indelibly labeled "Trotskyist," although I neither agreed with Trotsky's Marxism, nor ever shared the delusion that he might become the successful leader of a party. That the policies of Lenin and the original aims of the Bolsheviks were *defended* by Trotsky was made unmistakably clear in my little book, and will be unmistakably clear in history, I believe, if honest history survives. But my loyalty was not to any leader or group. My loyalty was still to the working class, to the idea of progress through class struggle. In principle I was merely supplying the international working class and its leaders with information essential to the intelligent conduct of the struggle.

With the same purpose I translated and published in 1928 the suppressed program and documents of the exiled Left Opposition of the Russian Communist party, calling the book *The Real Situation in Russia*. As the text was theirs rather than mine, I gave the royalties to a small branch of the Trotskyist Opposition which had by that time been formed in

America. This added to a growing impression that I was a
personal follower of Trotsky, although my private thoughts
about his failure to outmaneuver Stalin were anything but
those of a follower.* It was always Lenin's policies, and the
truth about what was happening in Russia, that I was defending. My translation of Trotsky's *History of the Russian
Revolution* was made with admiration but not endorsement.
To me that book is the supreme and most compelling application of the Marxian metaphysics to history, far outdoing the
similar efforts of Marx himself. But I think it will be the last.
No giant will ever again drive facts into those forms at such
an expense of intellectual power.

A book which marks a longer step in my own development, emotional if not intellectual, was my *Artists in Uniform*, written in 1932-33, and published in 1934. There I
described the hideous dictatorship in literature and the fine
arts set up under Stalin's knout, and the obsequious infan-
tilism of Americans like Mike Gold, Joe Freeman, Bob Mi-
nor, Hugo Gellert, Maurice Becker, William Gropper, my ex-
colleagues on the *Liberator*, who of their own free will
kneeled down to it. No one who had believed in the socialist revolution as a liberation of spirit, as we all in those
days so loudly did, could with intellectual honor pretend
that this was it or any step in the direction of it. I did not
pull any punches in that book, but I still spoke as a revolutionary socialist, a non-party old Bolshevik. I said in my
introduction:

"I am on the side of the Soviets and the proletarian class struggle. But I think that critical truth-speaking is an element of that
struggle essential to its success . . . The efforts toward socialist
construction in the Soviet Union must inevitably serve the world
movement in some sense as a guide. These efforts should not be

* They are described in the chapter, "Great in Time of Storm," of my book,
Heroes I Have Known.

followed, however, as a seamstress follows a pattern, but as a scientist repeats an experiment, progressively correcting the errors and perfecting the successful strokes."

Those were, I think, my last published words as a defender of the Soviet Union. It is not easy to set dates in such a matter. "Who can determine when it is that the scales in the balance of opinion begin to turn, and what was a greater probability in behalf of a belief becomes a positive doubt against it?" Cardinal Newman asks the question in his *Apologia*, and I must say that with all the documents I have in hand, I can not be exact as to the moment when I abandoned my attitude of "loyal to the Soviet Union but opposed to the Stalin leadership," and decided that thanks to that leadership the hope of socialism in Russia was dead. I only know that during the year 1933 those positive doubts grew so strong that I abandoned my pro-Soviet lectures, and remained silent for about two years. In the spring of 1936, I wrote an essay, "The End of Socialism in Russia," which was published in *Harper's Magazine*, January 1937, and afterward by Little, Brown & Company as a book. "To my mind there is not a hope left for the classless society in present-day Russia," I said in that book. But I still regarded Stalin's totalitarian dictatorship as an enemy, rather than a result, of the policies of Lenin.

It took me another two years to arrive at the knowledge that Lenin's methods—or in other words bolshevik Marxism—were to blame. This further slow step in my enlightenment was recorded in another book, published in 1940, and called *Stalin's Russia and the Crisis in Socialism.*

"I now think," I wrote in that book, "that this brilliant device for engineering a seizure of power, invented by Lenin with a super-democratic purpose, has shown itself to be in fatal conflict with the purpose. I think that an armed seizure of power by a highly organized minority party, whether in the name of the Dictatorship of the Proletariat, the Glory of Rome, the Supremacy of the Nordics, or any other slogan that may be invented, and no matter how ingeniously integrated with the masses of the population, will normally lead to the totalitarian state. 'Totalitarian state' is merely the modern name for tyranny. It is tyranny with up-to-date technique. And the essence of that technique is a reverse use of the very thing upon whose forward action Lenin ultimately relied, the machinery of public education."

This change of opinion invalidated much that I had said in the second part of my book, *Marx and Lenin, the Science of Revolution.* Moreover I had learned a great deal more about Marxism since that book was published in 1926. Its demonstration of the unscientific, and indeed superstitious, character of Marx's whole mode of thought seemed more and more important as the battle between the Soviets and western civilization developed. It was my main contribution to the battle, and I wrote it over again as maturely and carefully as I know how. With the title *Marxism Is It Science,* it was published in the autumn of that same year, 1940.

Even then, although rejecting Lenin's system of party control, I had not decided that "the socialist hypothesis" was disproven. That decision, or the inner force to confront that fact, arrived in the following year. And in this case I do remember the precise moment. At a cocktail party given by Freda Utley—I think for her friend Bertrand Russell—during a conversation about some last and most significantly dreadful news that had come out of Russia, she suddenly asked me:

"Aside from these Russian developments, do you still believe in the socialist idea?"

I said, "No."

Although I had never said this to myself, the answer came from the depths of my heart and mind. It seemed perfectly clear, once the question was boldly put, that if the socialist hypothesis were valid in general, *some tiny shred* of the benefits promised by it would have appeared when the Russian capitalists were expropriated and production taken over by the state, no matter how untoward the circumstances. By that time *everything* in Russia was worse from the standpoint of socialist ideals than it had been under the regime of the Tsar. I did not need any additional experiments such as that in Nazi Germany, or in England, or the obvious drift in other countries, to convince me. I was sure that the whole idea of extending freedom, or justice, or equality, or any other civilized value, to the lower classes through common ownership of the means of production was a delusive dream, a bubble that had taken over a century to burst.

I have never had any hesitations or regrets about the decision—only about the unconscionably long time it took me to reach it. When I am denounced as a turncoat by the true believers it does indeed bring a blush to my cheek, but only because it took me so long to turn my coat. I sadly regret the precious twenty years I spent muddling and messing around with this idea, which with enough mental clarity and moral force I might have seen through when I went to Russia in 1922.

This present book contains my principal conclusions, or the principal things I have learned politically, since making that decision. I imagine some of its readers will echo the remark of Upton Sinclair in a recent letter, that I have merely "gone from one extreme to the other." I think, on the contrary, that the step is shorter from hard-headed class-struggle socialism to a firm defense of the free-market economy than to the old wishful notion of a highminded slide into utopia.

It is a straighter step to take. The struggle is still for freedom; the main facts are still economic; the arch-enemy is still the soft-headed idealist who refuses to face facts.

My essay-chapters have been written at different times, and not always with a definite sequence in mind, but I think they follow each other in an acceptable order. I have to thank the *New Leader,* the *Freeman,* the *Reader's Digest,* and the *Saturday Evening Post* for publishing some of them, or parts of them, in advance.

MAX EASTMAN

January 1955

Part One

BOTH HOPES ARE FALSE

Chapter One

Almost everyone who cares earnestly about freedom is aroused against the Communists. But it is not only the Communists, it is in a more subtle way the Socialists who are blocking the efforts of the free world to recover its poise and its once-firm resistance to tyranny. In Italy, by voting with the Communists, they ousted De Gasperi's strong and wise government, and they are keeping his successors weak through the menace of similar action. In France, by refusing hearty collaboration with "capitalist" parties, they have made it impossible to form any stable government at all, producing just that chaos which the Communists desire. In Germany, after doing their best to oust Adenauer and his brilliant Minister of Economics, Ludwig Erhard, who accomplished almost single-handed "the miracle of German recovery," they are as this is written opposing his plan of rearmament, which offers the sole hope of effective West European resistance to an invading Communist army. In England they made a recovery like that of Germany impossible; their government recognized Communist China; and they are pushing to confirm for all time the Communists' hold on the impregnable land mass, or planetary fortress, of Eurasia. In Norway they have produced the closest imitation of an authoritarian state to be found this side of the iron curtain.

In America we seem remote from all this, but it is only because the Socialists in large numbers have abandoned the party label, adopting the Fabian policy of infiltration in other groups. Norman Thomas has withdrawn from the party executive and no longer functions as a political leader. Maynard Krueger, once candidate for Vice President on the Socialist ticket, resigned from the party, explaining that he did so not because his beliefs had changed, but because he thought devout American Socialists should associate themselves with the "liberal-labor coalition inside and just outside the Democratic party." This liberal-labor coalition has already transformed the Democratic party from an organ of Jeffersonian resistance to centralized power into the recognized advocate of increasing state control. It played a major part in the follies of Yalta, Teheran, Potsdam, and the China Story, which gave away well-nigh half the world to the Communists.

Thus in America as elsewhere it is the socialist ideal, as surely as the communist implementation of it, that is working against freedom. To thoughtful Americans Lenin's notion that a tiny group of detached zealots calling themselves the vanguard of the working class, after seizing the power and "smashing the bourgeois state," could establish a dictatorship of the proletariat—or any dictatorship but their own—has grown to seem preposterous. And the belief that such a dictatorship, having taken charge of the economy of a country, could lead the way to a classless society in which all men would be free and equal, is getting difficult even to remember. When remembered it is seen to be what it is—a dangerous fairy tale.

But we are still beguiled by this other fairy tale: that a large group of liberal-minded reformers, not pretending to be a class, not seizing the power but creeping into it, not smashing the state but bending it to their will, can take charge of the economy and approximate a free and equal society. This second notion is really more utopian than the first. The bolshevik scheme at least designated a social force which was to carry the process through. It looked scientific to say that the working class, once the existing order was smashed, would conduct the economy without paying tribute to capital, and a classless society would thus result from the natural instincts of men. The belief that such a millennium could be brought into being by "some combination of lawyers, business and labor managers, politicians and intellectuals," is hard to take seriously. And yet as Lenin's pseudo-scientific dream-hope evaporates, this more pure and perfect fantasy tends to take its place.

The phrase I quoted is from an essay contributed by Arthur M. Schlesinger, Jr., to a symposium on "The Future of Socialism," in the *Partisan Review* for May-June 1947. In that essay Mr. Schlesinger defined socialism in orthodox terms as "ownership by the state of all significant means of production," and declared it "quite practicable . . . as a long term proposition." He has said contrary things both before and since, and it appears that these words did not express a clear or firmly held opinion.* But that makes them all the

---

* The whole passage about how this "long term proposition" might be achieved reads as follows:

"Its gradual advance might well preserve order and law, keep enough internal checks and discontinuities to guarantee a measure of freedom, and evolve new and real forms for the expression of democracy. The active agents in effecting the transition will probably be, not the working class, but some combination of lawyers, business and labor managers, politicians and intellectuals, in the manner of the first New Deal, or of the labor government in Britain."

Mr. Schlesinger was quite savagely angry at me for quoting this passage correctly when the present essay was published in the *New Leader* (June

better illustrate the danger I am speaking of. For it is not the copper-riveted old-time believers in Marxian theory that we in America have to fear. Those old-timers, although calling themselves democratic, still give lip-service to the Marxian doctrine of progress through increasing class division. They do not seem to me really to believe in it any longer; in the present state of class relations in this country such a belief would require feats of mental gymnastics for which even Marx did not prepare them. But their formal adherence to this and the rest of the Marxian mystique isolates them in America. Their fairy tale is not plausible enough to be dangerous. It is the bureaucratic socializers—if I may devise that label for the champions of a lawyer-manager-politician-intellectual revolution—who constitute a real and subtle threat to America's democracy. It is their dream that is moving into focus as that of Lenin grows dim.

The assumption common to these two dreams is that society can be made more free and equal, and incidentally more orderly and prosperous, by a state apparatus which takes charge of the economy, and runs it according to a plan. And this assumption, though alluringly plausible, does not happen to be true. A state apparatus which plans and runs

---

1952). He thought I should have known that he did not mean what he said. "In order to chime with the purposes of the symposium," he explained, "I chose to write as if 'democratic socialism' and 'mixed economy' were the same. I made a mistake in so doing, as Mr. Eastman's confusion suggests. . . . . I am tired of Max Eastman and his present conviction that liberty resides in the immunity of private business from government control. I wish he would grow up . . ."

My "confusion" consisted in not having read Mr. Schlesinger's book, *The Age of Jackson* (1945), in which he "explicitly rejected the theory of socialism," nor yet *The Vital Center* (1949), in which he "explained his rejection of socialism at length."

I was indeed guilty of this confusion, but I have it now clear in my head that it was only during an interlude in 1947—a strange interlude, I must say —that Mr. Schlesinger came out explicitly for "ownership by the state of all significant means of production," meaning thereby a "mixed economy."

the business of a country must have the authority of a business executive. And that is the authority to tell all those active in the business where to go and what to do, and if they are insubordinate put them out. It must be an authoritarian state apparatus. It may not want to be, but the economy will go haywire if it is not.

That much was foreseen by many cool-headed wise men during the hundred-odd years since the idea of a "socialized" economy was broached. But the world was young, and the young can not be told—they have to learn by experience. (I was among the least willing to be told.) However, the actual experience of state-run economies, popping up one after another in the last thirty-five years, should be enough, it seems to me, to bring home this simple fact to the most exuberant. It is a fact which you can hardly fail to realize if you watch the operation of any big factory, or bank, or department store, or any place of business where a large number of people are at work. There has to be a boss, and his authority within the business has to be recognized, and when not recognized, enforced.

Moreover, if the business is vast and complex, his authority has to be continuous. You cannot lift him out of his chair every little while, tear up his plans, and stick in somebody else with a different idea of what should be done or how it should be done. The very concept of a plan implies continuity of control. Thus the idea that a periodic election of the boss and managing personnel is consistent with a planned national economy is lacking both in logic and imagination—you need only define the word "plan," or present a plan to your mind's eye. The thing is conceivable perhaps in a small enterprise, but where would you be if the nation's entire wealth production and distribution were a single business? Even supposing elections could be genuine when those in office controlled all the jobs in the country. Suppose they were genuine—you might as well explode a bomb under the economy as hold an election.

The phony elections in totalitarian countries, the ballots with only one party and one list of candidates, are not the mere tricks of a cynical dictator—they are intrinsic to a state-planned economy. Either phony elections or no elections at all—that is what thoroughgoing socialism will mean, no matter who brings it in—hard-headed Bolsheviks, soft-headed Social Democrats, or genteel liberals. Even now, with government handling only a third of our national income, it took the most popular candidate since George Washington to defeat the party in power. Even he could not carry in a Congress heartily in opposition. How could you unseat an administration with every enterprise and every wage and salary in the country in its direct control? Not only private self-interest would prevent it, and that would be a force like gravitation, but public prudence also—patriotism! "Don't change horses in midstream," we say. But we'd be in midstream all the time with the entire livelihood of the nation dependent upon an unfulfilled plan in the hands of those in office. "Don't rock the boat" would be the eternal slogan, the gist of political morals. That these morals would have to be enforced by the criminal law is as certain as that mankind is man.

FREEDOM AND THE PLANNED ECONOMY

Chapter Two

A FALSE and undeliberated conception of what man is lies at the bottom, I think, of the whole bubble-castle of socialist theory. Although few seem to realize it, Marxism rests on the romantic notion of Rousseau that nature endows men with the qualities necessary to a free, equal, fraternal, family-like living together, and our sole problem is to fix up the external conditions. All Marx did about this with his dialectic philosophy was to change the tenses in the romance: Nature *will* endow men with these qualities *as soon as* the conditions are fixed up. Because of his stress upon economic conditions, Marx is commonly credited with the cynical opinion that economic self-interest is dominant in human nature. Marx was far from a cynic about human nature. He believed that human nature is a function of the economic conditions, completely variable and capable of operating, once these conditions are "ripe," on the divinely rational and benign principle: "From each according to his abilities, to each according to his needs." It was to protect this optimistic dogma about human nature that the Stalin government felt obliged to stamp out the true science of genetics. According to that science, traits acquired during the lifetime of an organism are not appreciably transmitted in heredity. Only by selective breeding, whether artificial or natural, can profound changes be made in the nature of any species. While men's acquired characters may, and undoubtedly do, change with changing economic (and other) conditions, the underlying traits of human nature remain the same. There is little doubt that the Marxian bigots in the Kremlin were moved by this consideration in liquidating the world-famous geneticist, Avilov, and supporting the charlatan, Lysenko, in popularizing a belief in the wholesale heredity of acquired characteristics. Without such belief, the whole Marxian myth that economic evolution will bring us to the millennium falls to the ground.*

Once we have abandoned this myth, we can give heed to the real contribution of Karl Marx: his sense of the great part played by economic relations in determining political and cultural ways of life. His own sagacity will conduct us, then, to a genuinely scientific study of the economic foundations of political freedom. This study has been made by various economists of the "neo-liberal" school—Wilhelm Roepke, F. A. Hayek, Ludwig von Mises and others. Taking human nature as it functions in average life, they have shown that the competitive market and the price system are the basis of whatever real political freedom exists, or can be imagined to exist, where there is an elaborate division of labor.

---

* I pointed out this vital conflict between Marxism and modern science in my early book *Marx and Lenin, the Science of Revolution* in 1925, anticipating by twenty years—although far indeed from expecting—the physical liquidation of the scientists. The passage will be found unchanged in *Marxism Is It Science* (pp. 267-8-9).

The question of Marxism and the present conception of man is more fully discussed in my last chapter: "Socialism and Human Nature."

I am not an economist, but I have watched with some care the destinies of these men's earnest writings. There has been no answer, and I don't see how there can be an answer, to their assertion that mankind is confronted with a choice between two and only two business systems—a choice which involves the fate of democratic civilization. We can choose a system in which the amount and kind of goods produced is determined by the *impersonal* mechanism of the market, issuing its decrees in the form of fluctuating prices. Or we can choose a system in which this is determined by commands issuing from a *personal* authority backed by armed force. You cannot dodge this issue by talking about a "mixed economy." The economy is inevitably mixed; nobody in his right mind proposes a total abandonment of government enterprise. You can not dodge it by insisting the state must *regulate* the market or *intervene* in its operations. If carefully defined, that statement is obvious. The question is whether the economy is mixed to the point of destroying the essential directing function of the market, whether the regulations are a substitute for the market or a framework within which it shall operate, whether intervention is compatible or incompatible with the general control of the economy by the whole people as consumers of goods. That is the difference between collectivism and the market economy. That is the alternative with which mankind is confronted. You can not dodge it, or pray it away, or hide it from yourself with smokescreens of ideas. It is a fact, not an idea. We have to choose. And the choice is between freedom and tyranny.

There is no conflict between freedom so conditioned and a humane regard on the part of the state for people who fail utterly in the competitive struggle. No one need starve, no one need be destitute, in order to preserve the sovereignty of the market. The principle of collective responsibility for those actually in want can be maintained without violating the principle of competition. But we need no longer deceive ourselves that liberty in a human world is compatible with economic equality. Liberty means absence of external restraint. To democrats, it meant absence of arbitrary governmental restraint, and was to a degree synonymous with equality before the law. But to the Socialists it meant absence of all governmental restraint, and also of those more subtle restraints imposed by a minority who own the land and the wealth-producing machinery. Who, in the absence of these restraints, is going to impose equality? What is to bring it about that men, once granted leave to behave as they please, will behave as though the whole human race were a loving family? We have to make up our minds, if we are going to defend this free world against an oncreeping totalitarian state control, whether, in fact, our primary interest is in freedom from state control, or in an attempt at economic equality enforced by a controlling state. We have to accept such inequalities as are presumed by, and result from, economic competition.

Equality apart, however, there is something vitally democratic, as well as impersonal, in the control exercised by the market. When a man buys something on a free market, he is casting his vote as a citizen of the national economy. He is making a choice which, by influencing prices, will enter into the decision as to how, and toward what ends, the economy shall be conducted. His choice may be outweighed by others who buy more; that is inevitably true. But in placing the major economic decisions in the hands of the whole people as consumers, recording these decisions automatically through the mechanism of price, the market makes freedom possible in a complex industrial society. It is the only thing that makes it possible.

Strangely enough Marx himself as a historian was the first to perceive this. Looking backward, he observed that all our freedoms had evolved together with, and in dependence upon, private capitalism with its free competitive market. Had he been a man of science instead of a mystic believer in the inevitability of a millennium, he might have guessed at what is so clearly obvious now: that this dependence of other freedoms upon the free market extends into the future also. It is a brief step indeed from Marxism—once the Hegelian wishful thinking is weeded out of it—to such a passage as this from Wilhelm Roepke:

"It is hardly forgivable naïveté to believe that a state can be all-powerful in the economic sphere without also being autocratic in the political and intellectual domain and vice versa. . . . It therefore makes no sense to reject collectivism politically, if one does not at the same time propose a decidedly non-socialist solution of the problems of economic and social reform. If we are not in earnest with this relentless logic, we have vainly gone through a unique and costly historical object-lesson."

The failure of the Social Democrats, and still more in America of the "left" liberals, to learn this lesson is now a major threat to freedom in the western world.* I am not sure it is always a failure to learn. I think a good number of these Fabians and crypto-socialists—a new breed to which political expediency under the New Deal gave rise—have a suspicion that freedom will go down the drain. Travers Clement, one of the old-timers, has explicitly proposed hauling down the watchwords: "Liberty, Equality, Fraternity," and

---

* Sadly enough, the Social Democrats, though trained in "economic interpretation," are least of all able to learn this lesson. Even those emerging from their imprisonment in Marxian dogma take the wrong road. They reject what was sagacious and scientific about the master, his insistence on the importance of economic relations, and cling to his wishful dream, contradicted by all we now know about economics, of freedom under the planning state. Instead of going forward from their pseudo-scientific socialism to an expert, modern attempt to create a better society, they shrink back, clinging to a word and an emotion, into an attitude hardly distinguishable from that of the utopian socialists whom Marx superseded.

running up: "Cradle-to-grave Security, Full Employment and Sixty Million Jobs." * It was no accident of old age that both Sidney and Beatrice Webb and their brilliant colleague and co-evangelist in Fabian socialism, Bernard Shaw, ended their careers as loyal defenders of the most complete and ruthless tyranny mankind has known.

However, our American creepers toward socialism are most of them less bold and forthright than that. Often they don't even know where they are creeping. They see with the tail of an eye that political liberty is incompatible with economic subjection, but they refuse to look straight in the face of this fact. They refuse to learn the lesson that the history of these last thirty years has been spread out on the table, it almost seems, to teach them. They remain indecisive, equivocal—lured by the idea of security, orderly production, and universal welfare under a planning state, yet not quite ready to renounce in behalf of it those rights and liberties of the individual which stand or fall with the free market economy.

An ironical truth is that these socializers will not achieve security, orderly production, or the prosperity that makes universal welfare possible, by sacrificing freedom. They will be duped and defeated on all fronts. For me that also is proven by the history of the last three decades. But that is not the theme of this chapter.

Its theme is that our progress in democracy is endangered by democratic enthusiasts who imagine that they can preserve freedom politically while hacking away at its economic foundations. More even than the fellow travelers with their vicarious flair for violent revolution, or the Communists with their courageous belief in it, these piously aspiring reformers are undermining our hopes. Yearning to do good and obsessed by the power of the state to do it, relieved by this

* In the *New Leader* for August 4, 1945, answering my argument that democratic socialism is impossible.

power of their age-old feeling of futility, they are destroying in the name of social welfare the foundations of freedom.

Arthur Koestler warned us some years ago against the "men of good will with strong frustrations and feeble brains, the wishful thinkers and idealistic moral cowards, the fellow-travelers of the death train." We have accepted his warning. At least we have learned the meaning of the word fellow traveler, and are no longer falling in droves for these unlovely accomplices of the tyrant. We must arm our minds now against the less obvious, the more strong and plausible and patriotic enemies of freedom, the advocates of a state-planned economy. They are not on the train and have no thought of getting on, but they are laying the tracks along which another death train will travel.

THE REAL GUARANTEE
OF FREEDOM

Chapter Three

O<small>NE</small> of the unconscious mistakes of Socialists was to imagine that there is a beatific end, or any end at all, to human history. In the utopians this was excusable, for they were naively setting out to build an earthly paradise for man, and the idea could hardly occur to them that, once it was built, there was anything to do but live in it. When Marx breezed in, however, with his great brag of being realistic and hard-headed, telling us that ideals were unnecessary, the material universe is going "upward" eternally and the next stage after capitalism is bound to be socialism, it does seem odd that nobody asked: What comes after that?

Hegel has been smiled at for bringing the grand march of the Divine Idea in history to a sort of destination in the "practical and political condition existing in Prussia in 1821." Marx never joined in this smile. Marx scoffed at the Divine Idea, but took the grand march in history with monumental

36

seriousness. The absurdity of stopping a locomotive universe at the precise point where his revolutionary ideals were realized never occurred to him. Wishful thinking is too instinctive, especially among German philosophers, and Marx was too arrogantly adept at it. But if we are going to be seriously realistic, we'll have to make clear to ourselves that there is no end to the human journey. In our millennium we'll have to be content if things are "going well," and not ask them to exist fixedly, as heaven does, in a state of perfection.

Another mistake of the Socialists was to imagine that there might be brotherly peace in a free society—a settlement, that is, of all head-on conflicts of interest, all caste and class struggles. That might happen in heaven, but on earth men will always divide into groups with conflicting interests. As civilization advances they will divide into more groups perhaps, but not less keenly opposed. The task of the social idealist is not to suppress these groupings, or try to reconcile them, but to keep them in a state of equilibrium—never to let any one get out of hand. Our liberties depend upon the success of this effort. Only where every powerful group needs freedom for itself in order to compete with others can society as a whole be free. Freedom is the name of the arena in which various social forces contend.

Libertarians used to tell us that "the love of freedom is the strongest of political motives," but recent events have taught us the extravagance of this opinion. The "herd-instinct" and the yearning for paternal authority are often as strong. Indeed the tendency of men to gang up under a leader and submit to his will is of all political traits the best attested by history. It has been so shockingly exemplified in modern times that only a somnambulist could ignore it in trying to build, or defend, a free society. His first concern should be to make sure that no one gang or group—neither the proletariat, nor the capitalists, nor the landowners, nor the bankers, nor the army, nor the church, nor the government itself—shall have exclusive power.

This truth was apprehended by Plato and Aristotle, who preferred a "mixed constitution" in which a monarch, an aristocracy, and a popular assembly divide the power. For modern times it was formulated by the Italian, Gaetano Mosca, whose concept of an equilibrium of social forces seems actually to define the sole basis on which freedom can flourish.* Marx, of course, was untouched by such ideas. Marx was not a scientist thinking out the forms of a new society in which men might be happy, but a prophet announcing a millennium to follow the day of doom for the kingdoms of this world.

In sane good sense we radicals should have been thankful that, when the bourgeoisie displaced the feudal lords, a new class of proletarians was born, capable of sufficient organization to stand permanently against the bourgeoisie. We should count it a great folly in the advocates of proletarian revolution that they had in mind no other group, which, in the post-revolutionary society, might perform this indispensable function. "Permanent Class Struggle" would have been a wiser slogan than "Conquest of Power by the Working Class." For the idea that the victory of any one social force, whether you call it class, or vanguard of a class, or party, or executive committee, or politburo, or what you call it, could produce a "society of the free and equal," is the most fatal of Marxism's political mistakes. "Permanent Class Struggle" has, in fact, been the motto, or tacit assumption, of the American worker. And the American worker is far more sophisticated than the European, if only because he was too lazy to do his homework on *Das Kapital*. His mind is clear of a whole tangle of antique, animistic, and disproven notions.

* His book in the English translation is entitled, unfortunately, I think, *The Ruling Class*. It should be the *Political* or *Governing Class*.

"Permanent Class Struggle" was also the program Trotsky proposed to his followers in case the proletariat should not rise in victorious revolution at the end of World War Two. In a startling pronouncement, which his followers have been careful not to remember, Trotsky said:

"If [at the conclusion of this war] the world proletariat should actually prove incapable of fulfilling the mission placed upon it by the course of development, nothing would remain except openly to recognize that the socialist program based on the internal contradictions of capitalist society ended as a utopia. It is self-evident that a new minimum program would be required—for the defense of the slaves of the totalitarian bureaucratic society." *

For me there is a sorrowful irony in the fact that Trotsky, with whom I fought daylong over this question of Marxism versus experimental science, should have to confess from the grave that his beloved doctrine has been proven false by an experiment, and one that he himself had decided was crucial. The date he set for a showdown is ten years past, and the proletariat has dismally failed to fulfill its "mission." He believed, to be sure, that political democracy as well as socialism was doomed by this failure, but he could hardly postpone his "minimum program" until its doom was accomplished. He must needs have launched before now that struggle of permanent loyalty to the underprivileged which was all he had left.

He would have to humble his mind still more than that, however, if he wished to pursue in a world undistorted by Marxian superstition the ideal of a free society. He would have to recognize that other basic conflicts of interest, not just that between capital and labor, must be regarded as permanent. He would have to abandon that identification of self with the working class—a sentimental pretense not hard

* *The New International,* November 1939.

for an honest mind to abandon—and recognize that the champion of freedom stands somewhat apart from all social conflicts. His duty to plunge in on one side or the other is conditioned by time and circumstance. The sole fixed aim is to maintain an equilibrium—never to let any one force gain overwhelming power.

This will apply as much to the trade-union bureaucracy— and conceivably even to the trade-unions themselves—as to the bosses of industry and money. No man with his eyes open can fail to see that in the United States the power of the captains of organized labor is growing to a point where it should be regarded as a potential threat to freedom. Even the once-individualistic farmers have organized a pressure group that may have to be leashed, or balanced off, in the cause of a free republic.

It is an old question how much the course of history can be influenced by thoughts in the minds of men. Certainly it can be influenced in behalf of freedom only if thinking men learn to shift their attack from one threatening concentration of power to another. They will have to learn to change their aims—and what is more difficult, their allies—as the conditions change.

Though this will be hard for Marxists to learn, it is only a complete growing to maturity of that "flexibility" which was so prized by Lenin, and so brilliantly exemplified by him. Lenin called his rare gift "dialectic thinking," and imagined that it flowed from a belief that the material world is evolving toward his ideals in a zigzag fashion. Each thing turns someday into its opposite, the two are reconciled someday in a "higher unity," which again someday turns into its opposite, and so on forever—or at least until the believer gets where he wants to go. This supra-logical contraption is needful only to a man who has read his purpose into the evolution of the external world. He is tied by that act to the objective process unless he conceives the world as going forward by a series of intrinsically unpredictable sideways jumps. In short, the notion of dialectic enables the believer to escape in practical action from the rigidity that his theoretical faith imposes. That is its sole value to Marxists. Lenin was more accurate than he knew when he cried: "Flexibility of conception, flexibility to the point of the identity of opposites—that is the essence of the dialectic." *

To a mind aware that history is not an escalator, and that no one knows where the objective facts are leading, flexibility is inculcated by the mere fact of change. It requires no metaphysical hocus-pocus to justify it. And it is attainable to a degree that Lenin, with his fixed faith in a millennium to be reached by "resolving the contradictions in capitalism," never imagined. I can see no course open to the disillusioned Marxist who remains loyal to his original ideals but to attain that genuinely scientific flexibility.

He will have to make one further reduction in his Marxian pride, however. He will have to recognize that in the dream world in which they conducted their famous sparring match, the anarchists had as important a piece of wisdom in their keeping as the Marxists had. For one of the social forces which must be held in leash if the libertarian equilibrium is to be maintained is the political government. The anarchist idea that the state is the sole enemy, and that once the state is overthrown men will live instinctively in cooperative freedom, was childish indeed. It was a good deal more simply and lucidly childish than the imposing intellectual structure with which Marx tried to read his youthful passions into history. But when the balance is struck it will be found that Bakunin's criticism of the Marxists, and that of the less famous Russian Machaisky, were as valid as Marxism.

* "Thoughts on the Dialectic While Reading Hegel," Leninsky Sbornik V, IX, p. 71.

The state occupies a special position in society because it has a monopoly of armed force, but that only makes it more vital that it should not be sacrosanct. Not only must the power of the government be limited by law if the citizens are to be free—that too was known to Plato and Aristotle— but it must be limited by other powers. It must be regarded as but one of those social forces upon whose equilibrium a free society depends. When the state overgrows itself, the attitude of the anarchists becomes, within sensible limits, relevant and right; just as when the bankers swell up and presume to run a country, the attitude of the Marxists, barring their claim to universal truth, is right.

The last forty years of American history provide an excellent example of the manner in which developing facts demand flexibility in the fighter for freedom. During twenty of those years the fight was against something which may, for purposes of convenience, be called "Wall Street" or "Big Business." Nobody who engaged in the struggle to unionize the steel workers, or in the strike against the Rockefeller interests centering in Trinidad, Colorado, or who backed the Industrial Relations Commission of 1913-15, or the congressional investigation that called old J. P. Morgan on the carpet, need feel that his efforts were wasted. They were directed against the main enemy of freedom. But that enemy has been defeated and the battle won. Around 1930 the United States government began telling the financiers and captains of industry, instead of asking them, what to do.

I was informed by one of the biggest of these captains that the change occurred in the presidency of Herbert Hoover. He related to me how, at the beginning of the crisis of 1929, Hoover summoned to the White House the heads of fifteen or sixteen dominant industrial and financial institutions, and while they sat listening respectfully, told them that in spite of the break in the stock market, which would indicate a contrary policy, he wanted them to continue their expenditures for expansion and increased business. To use my informant's words as well as I can remember them: "We filed out obediently and went home and did what he told us to. And that night I made a note among my private papers, 'This day marked a turning point in the history of the United States.'"

The changing power-relations indicated in that meeting were carried to completion in the ensuing twenty years. The labor unions, or their officialdom at least, rose to the position of a major social force. In alliance with them the government took over the power from "Wall Street" or "Big Business" or the "Economic Royalists."

Stuart Chase, a pretty sharp-eyed referee in these battles, announced the victory in 1942. "Big Business," he said, which "dominated the official government, both federal and local, in the 1920's," has, since the depression "retired to the sidelines, and in some cases to the doghouse." The talk about "voracious bankers, outrageous profits, Sixty Families, greedy imperialists, wicked tycoons [is] on the futile side, if not approaching pure nonsense." The class struggle doctrine has been twisted by "the march of history" into "a hopeless wreckage." *

These lines, besides describing the facts with not too much exaggeration, expressed a general conviction among what Chase calls "socialist liberals." But neither he nor they realized what this meant, or should mean, to those interested in a free society. Instead of seeing and defining the new menace of overgrown power, ensconced now in Washington, not Wall Street, they went right on fighting the defeated enemy and boosting the victorious power.

* My quotations from Chase are from an article in *The Progressive* for October 12, 1952, "The Hour Gets Later and Later," and from "The War of Words," published almost simultaneously in *Common Sense*.

"The American community must submit to government and discipline if it is going to survive," Chase said. "There is no path to the nineteenth century and the old frontier." In war and peace we must have a "strong government," "a strong executive arm." "As a people we had better start to-morrow morning identifying the federal government at Washington with ourselves . . ."

This disaster need never have happened, had there been a general understanding of the conditions of freedom. The best of the "socialist liberals" are leading us in the direction of the slave state only because they have the idea of a fixed destination, and don't know where else to find it. Nothing is fixed; there is no destination. The task is to keep pace with history. The ideal is not peace but balanced conflict. Detached idealists of freedom should regard themselves as a mobile force in defense of the social equilibrium. Their aim at all times should be to prevent the domination of society by any one organized idea or power.

REPLACEMENT FOR THE DREAM WE LOST

Chapter Four

It was natural that idealistic people who had ceased to believe in heaven should think up some bright hope for humanity on earth. That, I think, more than any objection to "capitalism," accounts for the spread of the socialist dream, especially in Anglo-Saxon countries. During the nineteenth century, "capitalism" so-called raised the real wage of the British worker 400 per cent; the average real wage of the American worker rose, between 1840 and 1951, from eighteen to eighty-six cents an hour. A good fairy could hardly have worked faster. Of course it was not "capitalism" that did this; an abstract noun can't do anything. It was just the spontaneous way of producing wealth with elaborate machinery and a high division of labor. The word "capitalism" was invented by socialists for the express purpose of discrediting this natural behavior, and apart from the contrast with their dream it has no precise application. We should talk more wisely if we dropped this facile ab-

45

straction altogether, and made clear in each case what, specifically, we are talking about.

Especially we should invite down to brass tacks anyone who tells us "capitalism is doomed." That sonorous maxim is an intellectual scarecrow set up by socialists to frighten those who have wakened from their dream and are trying to find the way home to reality. It is just the same dream turned inside out. Even George Orwell, who depicted so brilliantly the horrors of what he called "oligarchical collectivism," was deceived by this maneuver. He was on the road home, but found these solemn words in his mouth: "Capitalism itself has manifestly no future." Meaningless words! And so he turned back, and died gazing at the dream, now mournfully dubious on the far horizon, that some other kind of collectivism besides oligarchical might come to be.

"I can't see any other hopeful objective," was the extent of his enthusiasm for the cause.*

It is not easy to let go of an idea around which one has organized a lifeful of emotions. On all sides one can see the lax yet still grasping logic of minds that once had a firm and flourishing hold on socialist belief. They are mainly concerned now to save face with their own pride. Somehow to keep the word and the feeling after the *plan* is abandoned —that inwardly is their problem.

It was tackled long ago by Georges Sorel with his doctrine of the "social myth"—an idea not valid, but necessary to set the masses in motion. Then came Hendrik de Mann with his discovery that "the present motive, not the future goal, is the essential." And now Sidney Hook finds "the day-by-day struggle for human decency and a better social order . . . more important than the 'ultimate' victory of a total program." Norman Thomas, in his rather pathetic *Demo-*

---

* The quotations are from an article on "The Future of Socialism" in *Partisan Review,* July-August 1947.

cratic Socialism, A New Appraisal (1953), throws overboard
everything that gave distinct meaning to the word socialism,
but continues to drive along in the old bandwagon with the
name printed on it in large letters. "Socialism will do this.
. . ." "Socialism will do that. . . ." he prophesies, naming
a variety of moderate reforms, forgetting that according to
his new appraisal socialism is nothing but a collective name
for these same moderate reforms. Ethically, to be sure, it is
something more—a society in which the spirit of mutual aid
predominates over that of competition—but how does that
differ from what he preached as a Christian minister before
his conversion to socialism? Another scheme for backing part
way out of the real meaning of socialism is to bring it all
down to supporting the cooperatives—a good thing to support, for they by-pass the state. But to be socialist, the cooperatives must aim to comprise the whole national economy, and in that case they would not by-pass, but be the
state. "The blending of parliament and the cooperative union
of Manchester must take place!" cried Ramsay MacDonald
in a debate with Hilaire Belloc in the days when socialism
meant socialism.

Today everybody is hedging. Even the British Labor party
has in the last four years been drifting rather than driving
toward socialism. Nationalization was distinctly played
down in the election campaign of 1951. Herbert Morrison,
speaking as a party leader in a keynote broadcast, said: "We
[and the Conservatives] believe in quite different economic
systems. We believe in full employment and the planning
necessary for it. The Conservatives do not." G. D. H. Cole,
the ardent Chairman of the Fabian Society, wrote in 1949:
"The administration of the few industries that have already
been transferred to public management is not yet so satis-
factory as to encourage a general adventure into industrial
socialization until the difficulties have been straightened

out, and more decentralization and more workers' partici-
pation in their affairs effectively introduced." In the days of
genuine socialist belief, nationalization and socialization
were almost interchangeable terms. Today "socialization of
the nationalized industries" has become a popular slogan
among British socialists." * The *New Fabian Essays* (1952)
compare with the old as the knitting of a tired grandmother
with the sprouting of a plant. Three of them, as Clement
Attlee concedes in a preface, "deal with the problem of making democracy effective in a society where managerial autoc-
racy is an increasing danger." With that danger increasing,
the zeal for a "gradual approach to socialism" is naturally in
sad decline. The wonderful merits of gradualness are no
longer so obvious.

It is better to be courageously humble about this and ad-
mit frankly that socialism was a mistake. An hypothesis
proven false, I call it for my own pride's sake. But whatever
we call it, let's get it out of the way of our minds. We have
the task of thinking out modes of dedication to a brighter
future for mankind that will not lead into the deepest pit of
darkness.

One thing we might do is to narrow the scope without
tainting the quality of our idealism—narrow it, I mean, both
in time and space. Perhaps it is a little grandiose to undertake to mold all history and a whole planet on the lines of
our ideal. Perhaps we are slightly infatuated these days
with globalism and historicism. I think in the future a good
many people who were, or might have been socialists, are
going to take a neighborhood for the scene of their effort, or
some single measure of assured benefit to mankind for its
scope. And I am not sure they won't be the happiest, as well
as the most useful, of these idealists—provided they can

---

* See "Socialism and the British Labor Party" by Leon D. Epstein in the
Political Science Quarterly for December 1951.

avoid the prying and authoritarian self-righteousness of the professional do-gooder. Real progress is piecemeal, and perhaps it would move faster if each community, or each generation, were to bite off a relatively small piece. Alexander Herzen remarked a century ago (as though foreseeing the Bolshevik debacle): "A goal endlessly remote is not a goal, if you please, but a hoax. The goal must be nearer. The goal for each generation is itself."

However, such wisdom is no substitute for the dream of a future paradise on earth. We have a right to dream. We have a right to make a big try. Only our dream must not be inconsistent with present measures that we can see in a shorter perspective are good. We must make sure that while we think we are marshaling mankind for a "leap from the Kingdom of Necessity into the Kingdom of Freedom," we are not actually leading him down the old well-paved road to serfdom. In short, if we are going to dream, let's dream in the right direction.

Taking human nature as it is, and accepting the indubitable necessity of private property and a competitive market if men are to be free, what should be the leading feature of a fair and true society? Here I am afraid that, besides lowering our banners, we shall have to creep back somewhat ignominiously into our belligerent past, and confess that one of our most triumphed-over opponents was right. Indeed I do not know any argument in opposition written during the high tide of socialist propaganda more precisely right than Hilaire Belloc's *The Servile State*. His prophecies have an accuracy that seems almost uncanny when you reflect that they were published in 1912—so long before two world wars reminded us what men are really made of. He asserts categorically, as though he had lived through it, that "at its first inception all Collectivist Reform is necessarily deflected and evolves, in the place of what it had intended, a new thing: a society wherein the owners remain few and wherein the proletarian mass accept a security at the expense of servitude." And he repeats as the kernel of his thesis:

"The Capitalist state breeds a Collectivist theory which *in action* produces something entirely different from Collectivism: to wit, the Servile State."

Although collectivist theory was far from popular at that time, Belloc was aware that the transition to collectivism was going to appear more "practical," and therefore be easier of achievement than the attainment of real blessedness in what he called the Distributive State. He was not an optimist about the Distributive State, but he was categorically sure that no third alternative exists.

"A society like ours, disliking the name of 'slavery' and avoiding a direct and conscious re-establishment of the slave status, will necessarily contemplate the reform of its ill-distributed ownership on one of two models. The first is the negation of private property and the establishment of what is called Collectivism: that is, the management of production by the political officers of the community. The second is the wider distribution of property until that institution shall become the mark of the whole state, and until free citizens are normally found to be possessors of land or capital, or both."

There is a radical ideal here, and a crisp and simple logic, that should give light—if their eyes can still stand it—to those semi-ex-socialists now blindly groping their way out of the maze of Marxian theory and emotion. I can add nothing to it, except my customary reminder that the basic error in the whole century-long blunder has been a crude and foolish conception, or no-conception, of human nature. The socialist idea was dreamed up by intellectual and radical-minded people, who constitute a very small and not typical section of the human race. You might almost describe the socialist movement as an effort of the intelligentsia to put over their tastes and interests upon the masses of mankind. I remember how when I traveled in Russia in 1922, long before I had waked, or knew I was waking, from the socialist dream, a certain thought kept intruding itself into my mind. These millions of poor peasants whose fate so wrings the heart of Lenin have only two major joy-giving interests outside their bodies and their homes: the market and the church. And Lenin, devoting his life selflessly to their happiness, has no program but to deprive them of these two institutions. That is not quite the way to go about the business of making other people happy.

We Socialists were, I think, profoundly wrong to ignore the depth and generality of the drive toward property, and therefore exchange of property, in man. Walt Whitman was profoundly wrong when he said in his famous hymn of praise to the animals: "Not one is demented with the mania of owning things." Ownership is not a mania, but a robust instinct extending far and wide in the animal kingdom. Even the birds stake out with their songs an area that belongs to them, attacking fiercely any intruder upon it. Less lyrical beasts serve notice by depositing distinctive odors on the boundaries of their domain. People who keep watch dogs can hardly deny the range and ferocity of the proprietary instinct. It was fully developed even among the nomads with their tents of different sizes. For settled and civilized man, there can never be a paradise, I fear, or even a sane and peaceful habitat, where this deep wish is unsatisfied. It has been neglected in utopias because their authors were guided rather by the Christian evangel of sainthood than by a study of the needs of average men.

It is not easy in America, where mass production has crowded people into vast industrial cities, to imagine each citizen as a landed proprietor! The dream is easier in Switzerland where factories are scattered through the country and average industrial workers quite normally own a home and a plot of ground. There is plenty of land here, however, and good reason, if only in the atom bomb, for scattering factories through the country. I see no reason why this more enchanting aspect of the distributive state should be ultimately and forever unattainable. And that free American citizens should normally be found possessors of capital, or property in the means of production, seems to me not only possible, but, granted two conditions are met, in the long run probable.

One of those conditions is that the idea of collective ownership, and all the distortions of fact which it produced in the minds of democratic idealists, be heartily abandoned. Most vicious of those distortions is the belief that "capitalism" imposes an "increasing misery" upon the working class. It is not enough to recognize, as all now do, that this Marxian prediction which rested on nothing but Hegelian dialectic, was false. We must recognize that the extreme opposite is true. Though it led off with the new-fashioned sufferings described by Marx in *Das Kapital*—not greater in degree, but different in kind from what had preceded—the market economy he thundered against has, in its full development, lifted the toiling masses of mankind to levels of life never dreamed of in all past history. It is only the habit of comparing reality with perfection instead of with what is possible, a habit proper to juveniles and fanatics, that blinds us to this. Whether or not it is true, as Von Mises asserts, that "capitalism . . . deproletarianizes all strata of society," * it is at least true that it makes possible their deproletarianization.

Let us suppose that the rate of increase in real wages mentioned in my first paragraph continued for another hundred

* *Human Action,* p. 665.

years. And let us suppose that throughout that new hundred years the radical idealists replaced their old zeal for collective ownership with as burning a zeal for universal individual ownership. Is it fantastic to imagine that they might bring on the day when "free citizens are normally found to be possessors of land or capital or both?" They would not at least, because infatuated with perfection, abandon the road of the general rise of income which makes such a thing possible. They would be dreaming in the right direction.*

In my opinion, however, no dreams whatever, and no plans even for a slightly better society than we have, will be realized unless the rise in wealth production is matched by a decline in the production of people. We shall have to go back farther than Belloc, we who have broken with socialism in the radical way we espoused it. We shall have to go back to Malthus, who perceived before socialism was born, the basic fact which foils all dreams of a just and generous society. There are too many people in the world; their number, when conditions are favorable, increases too fast. One of the worst effects of the Marxian religion of salvation by economics was that it swept this biological truth out of the minds of reformers and revolutionists alike. It belongs at the top of humanity's agenda.**

* The identical dream, by the way, is proposed as an immediate political program by the German-Swiss economist, Wilhelm Roepke. "If there exists such a thing as a 'social' right," he says in *Civitas Humana* (p. 257 of the French edition), "it is the right to property. And nothing better illustrates the confusion of our epoch than the fact that up to now no government, no party, has inscribed this device on its banner. If they think it would not be a success, we believe they are profoundly mistaken."
** In a book called *The Road to Abundance*, which I helped a chemical genius, Dr. Jacob Rosin, to write, the opinion is advanced that synthetic chemistry, or rather physico-chemistry, can solve all man's problems, including this one of population, by making him independent of both plant and mine. It is an exciting book with vitally important things to say. But I have my reservations about it—especially on this population problem which, even if all Dr. Rosin's other prophetic visions came true, would only be postponed.

There are many truths in this book which I have been lamentably slow to discover, but this I am happy to say is not one of them. From the beginning of my days as an agitator for socialism I warned of the priority of this problem. At the height of the exaltation of belief caused in me by the Bolshevik Revolution and a first glimpse of the writings of Lenin, I wrote:

"In Lenin's discussion of means for increasing the productivity of labor, I miss a reference to the means of decreasing, and intelligently controlling, the production of people. . . . The socialist movement will surely before long awake to the enormity of the population problem, and I can not but wish the awakening might be now, and in Russia, where the tendencies of the movement in the immediate future are to be crystallized." *

I was deceived about Russia. I was deceived about Lenin. I was deceived about the socialist movement. It never did awake to the importance of this problem. Such problems lie outside the universe of discourse in which socialism draws breath. As I have awakened from socialism, however, the problem has loomed steadily larger to me, and I must say, darker. It has been lightened in recent years by the anxious attention that has been drawn to it both among political scientists and among those engaged in physiological research. The Report on "The Determinants and Consequences of Population Trends," published by the United Nations on May 3, 1954, was a grim reminder of what is in store for us if we do not confront it. A great hearty and worldwide campaign of education might, it seems to me, after a long time, reverse the fatal trend of the statistics. Next to defending the free market, that seems to me the most important task that one still actuated by the wish for a more ideal society

* *The Liberator,* October 1918.

and still radical—radical enough to tear up the blueprints and begin over—could undertake.

More goods and fewer people is the slogan I should like to see carried at the head of humanity's march into the future.

THE DELINQUENT
LIBERALS

Chapter Five

THOSE who cling to socialism often say that we who have let go are suffering from shock at the murderous outcome of Lenin's seizure of power in a backward country. Having never backed Lenin, they are immune to this hysterical reaction and are calmly awaiting the emergence of socialism in its proper time and place. It is true that the horrendous results of Lenin's experiment in state control —and no less Hitler's—have influenced our judgment. They have reminded us of certain hard facts of human history that in our infatuation with an ideal we had forgotten. And who will deny that the reminder has caused painful emotion? Who will pretend that, having watched at the cradle of a "society of the free and equal," and seen rise out of it the most absolute and bloody tyranny that history has known, he did not experience a devastatingly sad surprise? I must testify, however, that I was more surprised and saddened by the reaction to that tyranny of liberal minds in free countries than by the tyranny itself.

I had never looked for purposive intelligence to our American liberals and humanitarian reformers. Although socially in the old days the line between us was not firmly drawn, we were separated emotionally and intellectually by my belief in progress through working class struggle. Kidding the *New Republic* of Herbert Croly and Walter Lippmann from a class-struggle point-of-view was one of my pleasant pastimes as a socialist editor. The *Survey* and Villard's *Nation* I liked better, but I thought of them too as theoretical opponents. I called the editors and adherents of these papers "soft-headed idealists," by which I meant people who use their minds to mitigate the subjective impact of unpleasant facts instead of defining the facts with a view to drastic action.

> Mind's task is not to blur the real
> With mimic tints from an ideal,
> But change one into the other by an act.*

There occurred no change in my feeling on this subject when I abandoned the idea of proletarian revolution. I still think the worst enemy of human hope is not brute facts, but men of brains who will not face them. For that reason I had no high expectations of the liberal intelligentsia when it came to acknowledging that the "revolution of our times," as so far conceived and conducted, is, has been, and will be, a failure. I never dreamed, however, that they could sink to the depths of maudlin self-deception and perfectly abject treason to truth, freedom, justice, and mercy that many of them have reached in regard to the Russian debacle. That has indeed profoundly, and more than any other shock, whether emotional or intellectual, disabused me of the dream of liberty under a socialist state. If these supposedly elevated and detached minds, free of any dread, of any

* The lines are from the preface to my poem, "Lot's Wife."

pressure, of any compulsion to choose except between truth and their own mental comfort, can not recognize absolute horror, the absolute degradation of man, the end of science, art, law, human aspiration, and civilized morals, when these arrive in a far country, what will they be worth when the pressure is put upon them at home? They will be worth nothing except to those dark powers which will most certainly undertake to convert state-owned property into an instrument of exploitation beside which the reign of private capital will seem to have been, in truth, a golden age of freedom and equality for all.

To that much emotional shock I plead guilty. But I do not want to leave it there. Many of these delinquent liberals were my friends in past years despite our differences, and I find myself continually puzzling over the problem of their motivation. Why have they betrayed themselves? Why do they promote the interests of a regime under which even they, traitors to democracy though they are, would be shot for half-heartedness, or permitted to die of starvation in a slave camp for having in the past believed, or thought they believed, in freedom?

Up to the Bolshevik Revolution it is not hard to understand what happened to them. The old liberal movement grew out of the struggle against absolutism and feudal oppression. The freedom fought for in that struggle included free trade as a matter of course. But free trade and the industrial revolution soon raised the general wealth so high that idealists began to worry about the living conditions of the poor. Those living conditions were not, in the general average, worse than they had been. The change was in the attitude of civic-minded people toward them. It is not too much to say, as the canny Norwegian, Trygve Hoff, does, that a social conscience was born of this great rise in wealth production. The first sensible step toward bettering the general condition of the poor would obviously have been to increase still more the production of wealth. Then if the pangs of the social conscience had kept pace with this increase all might have been well. What these pangs did was to run way ahead of the increase in wealth. People were attacking the businessman and demanding a better distribution of profits long before such distribution would have made any appreciable difference in the general condition of the poor. As wealth production increased, this state of pained conscience among liberals—themselves businessmen often enough—increased much faster. So fast that their zeal for liberty was gradually replaced by a zeal for a more equal distribution of wealth. Their liberalism became almost indistinguishable from humanitarianism. And this change of mind and mood among liberals was certainly not retarded by Marx's doctrinaire announcement that their interest in freedom had been a fake all along: capitalist profits, not human rights, had been the goal of their struggle against absolutism; their great revolution had been "bourgeois," not democratic.

They still talked the language of liberty—so also did Marx —but their dominant drive was toward a more even-handed distribution of the unheard-of wealth that, under a regime dominated by the idea of liberty, had been piling up. The culmination of this change was, in England, the decline of the Liberal party, the seeping away of its membership into the Labor party with its promise to expropriate the capitalists, and in the United States the transformation of the old liberal press into organs of the New Deal—the government of settlement workers become militant, not in the cause of freedom, but in the battle against "economic royalists." The whole development is summed up in the contrast between Benjamin Franklin's: "Those who would give up essential liberty to purchase a little temporary safety deserve neither

liberty nor safety," and Harold Laski's: "Those who know
the normal life of the poor . . . will realize well enough
that, without economic security, liberty is not worth having."

This much, then, must be said in defense of the delinquent
liberals. The edge of their passion for freedom had been
growing blunter for decades before the rise of totalitarianism put their loyalties to a test. It is not only freedom that
they betray, however, in apologizing for the Soviet tyranny,
or pussyfooting about it, or blackening America so savagely that Russia shines in unspoken contrast. They are
betraying civilization itself. They are lending a hand in the
destruction of its basic values, promoting a return march in
every phase of human progress. Reinstitution of slavery, re-
vival of torture, star chamber proceedings, execution without
trial, disruption of families, deportation of nations, massacre
of communities, corruption of science, art, philosophy, history, tearing down of the standards of truth, justice, mercy,
the dignity and the rights of man—even his right to martyr-
dom—everything that had been won in the long struggle up
from savagery and barbarism. How shall I account for this
depraved behavior—for that is how it appears to me—on the
part of friends and colleagues who were once dedicated to
an effort to make society more just and merciful, more truth-
perceiving, more "free and equal" than it was?

They shield themselves from facts, I suppose, by a biased
selection of the books and newspapers to read. Many violent
conflicts of opinion come down to a difference in reading
matter. And this is especially so in the case of Soviet communism, for it has been put over with a campaign of All-
Russian and International Lying whose extent, skill, effi-
ciency, and consecration is almost harder to believe in than
the truth it conceals. Indeed the distinction between truth
and the exact fabrications handed down for propagation
by the heads of the world party in the Kremlin has disap-

peared very largely from the minds of its members. Until one has grasped this phenomenon in its full proportions, and learned to distinguish the sincere truth-teller from the sincere lie-teller, it is not easy to be hard-headed about Soviet communism. That too may be advanced in defense of the delinquent liberals—they are the victims of a swindle which nothing in past history had prepared them to detect.

A great many of them, however, are not deceived, but are swallowing the horrors of life under the Soviets with open eyes and a kind of staring gulp that is more like madness than a mistake. In the effort with their soft heads to be hard they have gone out of the world of reasoned discussion altogether. Again I will take the late Harold Laski as an example. No anti-communist has more candidly and crushingly described the blotting out of civilized values and all free ways of life by the Russian Soviet state than he did; and yet no pro-communist has more vigorously defended that state, or brought more intellectual authority to its support. There must be, I suppose, in all the delinquent liberals, a repressed conflict between the impulse to speak those truths that are important to man's civilized survival and the more compelling thirst for a comfortable opinion. In Laski, because of some strange and perhaps bumptious quirk in his nature, this conflict was not repressed, but was naively or insolently blared forth. I met him for the last time in a debate on the "Town Meeting of the Air" September 19, 1946. Knowing about this conflict in his soul, I brought with me, typed out in condensed form, the passage from his *Reflections on the Revolution of Our Time* in which he most eloquently describes the horrors of life under the Soviet communist regime.

In the course of the debate, I made a remark about the crimes of the Russian Communists, and Laski replied: "It's no part of my case that Russia hasn't committed crime and been guilty of grave blunders and committed inconceivable follies; so has the United States, and so has Great Britain."

In answer, I said: "I'm going to read you from Laski's own book some of the crimes that have been committed in the Soviet Union, and you see if any of them have been committed in the United States or England." I then read this passage from Laski's book, or as much of it as I could crowd into the time granted me.

"Despite the pledges of the Constitution of 1936, there is no freedom of speech, except for Stalin's adherents, no freedom of the press or assembly. Everyone knows that the elections are a farce; no candidatures are possible which reject the party line, and even the ballot-papers for them read like a hymn to Stalin. Freedom of movement is gravely restricted. Contact with foreigners is looked upon with suspicion. There is arbitrary arrest; there is long imprisonment and execution without trial. Citizens can not travel abroad without the permission of the government. Most political offences are tried in secret; there is no writ of *habeas corpus*, no right to subpoena witnesses, no right to a professional defence. The death-penalty may be imposed for injury to, or theft of, collective property; and even 'teasing, mocking, or persecuting' a shock-worker may, under Article 58 of the Criminal Code, become 'wrecking,' and so punishable with death."

The moderator interrupted me and asked Laski: "Do you care to comment?" And Laski, spreading his hands in a gesture which my friends in the audience described as sickly, answered:

"No."

Laski did have, of course, a scheme for convincing himself that in a nation so chained and trampled by power-lustful and unbridled masters of the state, the Revolution of Our Time is bringing to birth a new age of freedom and humane reform. He accomplished it by opposing the words "economic" and "political" as though they designated things happening on different planets. While the above listed horrors filled the sphere called politics, the sphere called economics, he asked us to believe, was brimming with sweetness and light. I quote, also with condensation, from the same book:

"In the narrow economic sphere, there is a more genuine basis for economic freedom for the masses in the Soviet Union than they have elsewhere previously enjoyed . . . Millions, in every field and factory, help to make the conditions under which they live. There are the effective beginnings of constitutional government in industry. The rules of an enterprise are not made at the discretion of an employer who owns it, but are genuinely the outcome of a real discussion in which men and management participate . . . Care for the health, sanitation, and safety of the workers in field and factory has been established at a pace which would have been unthinkable in any capitalist society. . . . The administration of justice (political offences apart) . . . is on a level superior to that of most other countries. . . . Bench and bar alike have a more active and sustained interest in the improvement of legal procedure than anyone has displayed in Europe since Jeremy Bentham."

It is obvious that no man thinking about concrete facts could put these two passages into the same book and chapter. How can it be that in a country where "there is no right of *habeas corpus,* no right to subpoena witnesses, no right to a professional defence," nevertheless "the administration of justice (political offences apart) is on a level superior to that of most other countries"? What jocular Deity brings it about that while death may be the penalty for teasing another worker, nevertheless "care for the health, safety and sanitation of the workers" outruns all previous norms? How does it come to pass that where "elections are a farce, freedom of movement is restricted, there is arbitrary arrest, imprison-

ment and execution without trial," nevertheless "there are
the effective beginnings of constitutional government in
industry . . . and millions help to make the conditions under which they live"? Would these millions not be more
likely, in a real world, to establish the beginnings of constitutional government by making the rules under which they
can be dragged out and shot?

That this artificial division of society into two halves, political and economic, in which opposite things are taking
place, should have been put before us with obeisances to
"Marxism," was a prodigy of intellectual acrobatics. Marx
might be said to have spent his life trying to forestall this
shallow dichotomy. But Marx or no Marx, any man of hard
sense knows that the Russian people are not being subjected
to those hideous political repressions for their own good. It
is not to bring in the Kingdom of Heaven that the masters of
the state have locked the population in this toothed vise.

I dwell upon this unreal notion of Laski's because I think
it exposes in a raw and yet elaborated form what has happened in the minds of many of the pro-Soviet liberals. They
are not totally blind to the monstrous things that have happened in Russia, but they have reasoned their way to a point
of tranquil acquiescence by means of this nonsense about
political versus economic.

This too, then, must be said in behalf of the delinquent
liberals: they had a rationalization, a cerebral alibi, so to
speak, for their crime of treason against civilization. They
managed to draw the whole thing up into their heads where
it did not seem so bad.

It is significant that while the pro-communist liberals apol-
ogize for the *political* enslavement of the Russian people on
the ground that they are *economically* free, the pro-socialist
liberals make an opposite use of the same artificial distinction. They tell us that *economic* enslavement will not deprive
us of our real freedom, which is *political*. Philip Rahv in the

Partisan Review, defending the British socialist regime against the assertion of Dos Passos that "personal liberty has been contracted in Great Britain," said: "The evidence cited by Dos Passos shows that the contraction he speaks of has occurred solely in the economic sphere. Socialists, however, do not consider the right to buy and sell as one pleases to be a significant part of the heritage of freedom." * Stuart Chase took the same line in defending a state-planned society, and to them both Friedrich Hayek made the obvious and conclusive answer: "Economic control is not merely control of a sector of human life which can be separated from the rest; it is the control of the means for all our ends." * *

It hardly requires a Marx or a Hayek, however, to reveal the unreality of this dichotomy. It is clear to all who possess "the faculty to imagine that which they know." And I often think that the lack of this faculty or habit, so justly praised by Shelley in his *Defense of Poetry,* is one of the main causes of the delinquency of the liberals. They are predominantly intellectual—and are not intellectuals in general, even when originally moved by sympathy, strangely heartless and conscienceless through the very fact that they make a habit of abstract thinking? A phrase like "workers and peasants," or "kulaks," or "prison camps," or "execution without trial," becomes a bloodless pawn which they move about on the cerebral blueprint of a schemed-out world with as little sense of the human hearts and bodies designated by it as though they were playing a game of chess. This enables them to go on calling themselves "left" and "liberal" after all the original meaning except to their own self-esteem has been drained out of those terms.

Another and cruder motive undoubtedly swung many once refined liberals into the camp of the brutalitarian tyrants. That is an underlying irresistible wish to associate

* "Disillusionment and Partial Answers" in *Partisan Review* for May 1948.
* * *The Road to Serfdom,* pp. 88 and 92.

themselves with power. Their early ideals had made spiritual rebels of them in their own country. They were commonly not only against the government and the "vested interests," but in a condition at least of mild demur against the whole established hierarchy of persons and values. To the thinking mind this was valid and exciting, but to mere organic tissue it was a hard attitude to keep up for a lifetime. All human history testifies to the strength and generality of what may be called the hierarchical instinct. Students of comparative psychology have found it to prevail rigidly even in so pre-human a society as is to be found in the henyard. The caste system in a colony of jackdaws, as described by Konrad Lorentz in his book, *King Solomon's Ring*, throws astonishing light on several traits and institutions that we think of as peculiarly human—particularly the disposition to recognize the elite, to fall in line comfortably under those having the prestige of superior power. Its roots seem to be as deep, almost, as the impulse to form a society. Surely this trait can not be ignored in trying to assess the causes of the cultural disaster that I am discussing.

Dwight MacDonald, speaking of a liberal whose delinquency was transitory and need not be advertised here, says: "The spell of communism for people like him seems to have been that at last they could identify themselves with power without feeling guilty. His political language, in America a despised minority dialect, was now spoken throughout a sixth of the globe. A vast international movement backed by a powerful government was going his way —or seemed to be."

Whatever may be the inner truth about the individual in question, the acuteness of this comment on the great wave of enthusiasm for "the proletariat" that struck our liberal intelligentsia in the early thirties, can not be denied. Why did not this wave arise in the early years of the Bolshevik Revolution, when, although violent and brutal deeds were done, they were unsystemized and unusual, and were matched by heroic strides toward ideal reform in almost every phase of life? Hardly a single one of the noted liberals who came so boldly to the defense of Stalin's matured and hardened totalitarian police state had a good word to say for the regime of Lenin and Trotsky. There was a hazard then. Later there was a settled and secure new form of power. It is hard to escape the conclusion that in the depth of them that is what they wanted.

Still I do not think this trait, or all the above traits together fully explain the treachery to civilization of so many distinguished minds in this crisis of man's history. They had not all lost their passion for freedom; they did not all fall for the lie campaign, or swallow the politics-versus-economics moonshine; they are not all excessively cerebral, or swayed by the primitive adoration of power. I think probably the most general explanation lies in a kind of spiritual cowardice. Life is a battle; it is a battle without any final or assured victory, and these aspiring idealists lack the pluck to go down fighting it. Bereaved of other-worldly goals, they have been yearning for some home, some certainty, some Absolute on earth, if it is only the absolute parody of their dreams. And that is about all there is left of the Soviet heaven after they get through listing the qualifications in their adoration of it. The extent of these qualifications makes plain the selfishness of their mental condition. With all their brains, they can not draw the inference that any casual man who cares about other people even a little bit must draw from the continuing horrors suffered by millions of simple-hearted, honest folk under the Kremlin's lash. They can not do it because it would cause a pain in their own safe bosoms. They would have to know, then, that the world is just as bad as it is, and just as fluid too. There is no end-term in the fight to better it.

WHAT TO CALL
YOURSELF

Chapter Six

ALTHOUGH it seems sad that intelligent crea-
tures can be so childish, I believe that the wish to be called
radical and regarded as belonging to "the Left" is a further
cause of the treachery to civilization of many liberals. It is
not concrete goods or values they are defending, but a
name, and a status corresponding to it, in the hierarchy of
political emotions. They fail to realize, or do not wish to, a
fact which Thucydides remarked upon two thousand years
ago: that in times of revolutionary upheaval words are
forced to change their meanings.* In discussing this, and
other more bloody violences committed by revolutionists,
Thucydides lays the worst blame upon "men who entered
the struggle not in a class, but in a party spirit." The remark
is peculiarly relevant in our times because the first and most
fundamental violence against language committed by the
Marxian revolutionists was to make *class* mean *party*. Marx

* *The Peloponnesian War,* Chapter X.

68

with his cryptic remark that "philosophers" instead of understanding the world ought to change it, and Lenin with his
more lucid assertion that the workers can not of themselves
arrive at a socialist consciousness, it has to be brought to
them by "bourgeois intellectuals," prepared the ground for
this operation. The term "working class" was detached from
the actual workers and attached to a party of believers in the
Marxian theory about what the workers were going to do.
This innocent-looking maneuver set the style for such etymological atrocities as calling it "liberation" when the Red
Army marches in and arrests, jails, rapes, deports or shoots
30 per cent of a nation's population, and pinning upon the
resulting perfect tyranny the name of "People's Democracy."

These crude tricks of demagogues can with a trifle of in-
genuity be seen through. But they are only an artful exaggeration of natural tendencies that are more slow-moving,
more subtle, and more dangerous to the life of truth. The
word "left" has, over the last hundred years, gone through a
change quite as complete as that suffered by "liberation" and
"democracy" between Lenin's arrival at the Finland Station
and Stalin's extension of power to Eastern Europe and
Asia. In its beginnings, in the democratic revolutions of the
eighteenth and nineteenth centuries, this word designated
the people and groups who stood for the individual and his
liberties as against the "constituted authorities." In the
French National Assembly of 1789, the nobles still com-
manded enough respect to receive places of honor at the
right of the speaker, and the radicals naturally drew off as
far as possible to the other side. Seats in the center remained
for those having temperate views and emotions. In many
European parliaments the precedent thus established was
continued, and a distinction which had been specific and
ceremonial became universal and political. The nobles were
soon outside the building, but still on the right. The absolut-

ists of individual freedom, the anarchists, were outside too, but they were the "extreme left."

Whatever may have been the individual exceptions, there was little doubt about the meaning of these two terms. In Europe especially their connotations were extensive and very rich. The "man of the Right" was characterized in general by a taste for uniforms, badges, and emblems of hierarchical distinction. The "man of the Left" liked a plain suit of clothes, and the farther left the plainer and simpler, until you reached the soft collar and cap and loose flowing tie of the Bohemian rebel. The man of the Right liked titles and ceremonies; he addressed people with careful regard for the distance between them. He revered personages and looked down on mere human beings. The man of the Left shook hands and said hello to everybody, and why not? The man of the Right was for law and order as good in themselves. The man of the Left was for law primarily as a defense of the rights of the citizen and his liberties. The man of the Right was conventional and inclined to respect accepted opinions. The man of the Left was ready to kick over the conventions, and go in for independent inquiry on any subject. All these traits enriched the connotation of left and right, but most of all, and at the bottom of all, the attitude to the constituted authorities, to the state. "The individual on one side, the state on the other, that is the underlying substance of this contrast," says J. Pera in an engaging essay on this subject.*

Now it is clear that not only in their underlying substance, but in all their essential implications, these words left and right have exactly changed places. In America, and I think in all Western countries, a "leftist" is a man unhorrified by the Soviet tyranny and acquiescent in the gigantic overgrowth of the state at home. The restoration in Russia of

* *Études Matérialistes,* No. XIV, September 1947.

epaulettes, salutes, emblems, and attitudes of rank, the transformation of "comrade Stalin" first into "Marshal" and then
"Generalissimo"—even the adoption of the goosestep in the
Red Army—did not disturb his feelings. The reverence for a
personage passing almost into obeisance before a god was
not revolting to him. He accepted, or found excuses for, a
system of law which, instead of defending men's liberties,
was focused upon suppressing them, and where it failed of
that could be replaced by administrative decrees, or mere
decisions of the state police. Conventions made rigid; opinions handed down by infallible authorities; value judgments
made obligatory in every field of endeavor; a fixed hierarchy
of caste and imposed status in civil and industrial as well as
military and political life—all these things were meekly
swallowed down. In short, every judgment and choice,
every trait and mode of behavior, that once had given
meaning to the word "right" is now supported or condoned
by those whom all agree in calling "left" or "leftist."

This would not matter so much if it were clearly and
generally understood. But so much of the original magnetism
still inheres in the term "left"—some suggestion, at least, of
readiness for idealistic adventure—that to have it pinned on
them, many once stout-hearted liberals are now actually
willing to kneel down at the feet of the unqualified tyrants
enthroned in the Kremlin. The thing is intelligible to me because, having been all my life a man of the Left, and having
experienced no inner change or conversion, I find it almost
organically painful when someone alludes to my present political opinions as "rightist" or as representing "the Right."

This makes the problem what to do about the reversed
meaning of these key terms an acute one to me personally,
but I think it is also of public importance. There ought to be
some etymological device by which a person still bent on
defending the free individual against the encroachments of

a morbidly proliferating state can outmaneuver this trick that language and history, without any evil intention, have played upon him. Perhaps if we think out the manner in which the thing came to pass, some such device will occur to us. At any rate I am going to describe, as it appears to me, the process by which in the last hundred-odd years—that is, since the democratic revolution—the word left has come to mean right and the word right, left.

Modern democracy arose and has gone forward under a banner inscribed with two ideals: liberty and equality. They were combined in our Declaration of Independence. They were combined in the fighting slogan of the French Revolution, which became the motto of the French Republic. They are combined in all properly constituted Fourth of July orations. The phrase "free and equal" has been almost as current in America as the word democracy itself.*

To our forebears these two words had much the same meaning. Freedom meant electing your own government by popular vote; equality meant that each citizen has one vote. Freedom meant the rule of law; equality meant that all men are equal before the law. Freedom meant that there should be no publicly recognized social barriers; equality meant the same thing. There was no confusion here because life was simple, the earth roomy, and the talk mainly about politics. But when life became complex, crowded, *industrialized*, and we began to think in terms of economics, an inherent conflict between these two ideas emerged. It is quite obvious that if men are economically free, even in no absolute sense, inequalities will develop among them. And conversely, they can not be held to economic equality, or anything approaching it, without forcible restraints.

It was the Socialists who brought in the idea of extending

* See "Notes on the use of the word 'Democracy' " by R. R. Palmer, *Political Science Quarterly*, June 1953.

democratic ideals to the economic relations of men, and it was Marx who made this idea look practical, and indeed inherent in the natural development of economic relations. He proposed to make equality economic by abolishing the competitive market, and having all wealth produced and distributed by the state. Freedom, he promised, would follow of itself. After a transitional period of dictatorship, the state would, in fact, "wither away."

With that notion of a "transition" to the withering away of the state he concealed the inescapable head-on conflict between liberty and equality. He concealed the fact that, as between the two, he had chosen equality, not liberty—a classless society, to use his term—and was prepared to let the state do what had to be done to bring it into being. He concealed from the Left, or at least a major part of it, that he was a man of the Right—a Hegelian state-worshipper in his training, and in his instincts, as Bakunin described him, "a bourgeois through and through."

I do not mean to imply that Marx consciously concealed these facts, or that he was hypocritical about the withering away of the state. He believed in his wishful thought system with all the ardor of the typical German metaphysician. Lenin also believed in it. No one can read his pamphlet, *State and Revolution,* published on the eve of the October revolution, and his "program address" to the Soviets six months after it,* and have any doubt of his sincere faith in the promises of the dialectic universe. But he too was by temperament, except in his social habits, a man of the Right, a zealot of centralized authority and allegiance to it. In the heroic days of the seizure of power he rallied to his banner of transitional dictatorship the Left Social Revolutionaries, and even a few anarchists. But they soon saw what an instrument of regimentation, and what a regimented instru-

* I referred to this pamphlet on page 10 also.

ment, his party was. They withdrew and watched with dismay—those of them who were not imprisoned or executed—while he laid the foundations of a party-state which should become more meticulously authoritarian, and more contemptuous of the individual man and his freedoms, than any other regime in history.

I am, of course, greatly simplifying a complex ideological development. The thought of the Marxists was that political freedom meant freedom only for the exploiting classes, and their motive was to make all men *equally free*. But while this resolves in abstract logic the conflict between the two ideals, in practical action it resolves nothing, for the base of all freedom as now conceived is economic. It is economic equality—equality in relation to the all-determining enterprise of wealth-production—that is to "set the proletariat and therewith all society free." And this equality, as events have a thousand times proven, can not be established or maintained without newly devised, widespread, and violent restraints. With all the metaphysical casuistics, dialectic incantations, and earnest economic lucubrations he brought to the support of it, Marx's "society of the free and equal" is a contradiction in terms. In no conceivable society can men be in the economic sense both equal and free.

The gradual ascent into prominence of this submerged fact is the principal cause, I think, of the automatic change that has taken place in the meaning of such terms as left and right. No serious person outside Russia believes any longer in the withering away of the state. But the shift of attention from freedom to equality that was accomplished by that mythical invention, continues to prevail among our extreme democrats. They still wish, in varying degrees, to extend democracy into the field of economic relations, and they still take it for granted that democracy implies freedom as well as equality. No one of them has made a conscious choice between the two directive ideas: freedom from state control, and equality enforced by a controlling state. But unconsciously they have—partly under the influence of Marxism, partly of a new secular humanitarianism which replaces the churchly religion—plumped without reservation for the latter alternative. They are still to their own thought on "the Left," but their tolerance of centralized authority, of state rule over the will of the individual, exceeds, in many cases, that of the extreme right in the days when those terms first acquired a political meaning.

This poses a problem for all who prefer freedom to equality as a guiding idea, or who realize that economic freedom is essential to the maintenance of a high level of life. How shall they distinguish themselves in everyday parlance from their opponents on what used to be the Right? The word "left" is lost to them completely. Their natural recourse would be to the term "liberal," which when used historically designates correctly enough the heart of their position, its emphasis on free trade and a free market economy. But in political parlance this good word too is sliding over to the other side. Instead of meaning open-minded toward individual variation and disposed to curb authoritarian interference with it, "liberal," when not modified by a dexterously chosen adjective now means much the same thing as left. It most emphatically does not mean on guard against the spread of collectivist ideas and against state interference with a free market economy.*

A principal reason for this second change, it seems to me, is the optimism about progress prevailing in the nineteenth century and after. The liberals did not fall for the socialist

---

* "To lay the ghost at the outset and to dismiss semantics, a liberal is here defined as one who believes in utilizing the full force of government for the advancement of social, political and economic justice at the municipal, state, national and international levels." Joseph S. Clark Jr., Mayor of Philadelphia, in the *Atlantic Monthly*, July 1953.

panacea or bother with the myths of dialectic materialism, but they were confident in a less cerebral way that the world was traveling in their direction. Even so analytical a thinker as John Stuart Mill could remark that "a Liberal is a man who looks forward for his principles of government; a Tory looks backward." So it is not surprising that the average man, or at least the voluble man who moulds language, came to think of liberals as open-minded toward the future rather than committed to any present conception of life. To him, in the general atmosphere of optimism, the word meant "ready and eager to fall in with the march of Progress." Indeed the word liberal was at times abandoned—explicitly by the *New Republic,* I remember—and "progressive" adopted in its place.

But now this blind Victorian giant, "Progress," has led us into a tunnel with a black end, and those thoughtfully concerned about liberties have the hard task of turning around and finding the way back for a new start in the light. That is the simple and sorrowful truth. And meanwhile to the above average talker it still seems "liberal," as well as "progressive," to plunge on into the darkness.

Several attempts have been made to find an adjective capable of rescuing this precious word liberal and bringing it back toward its old meaning. Wilhelm Roepke describes the position taken in his admirable book, *The Social Crisis of Our Time,* as "liberal conservatism." In another passage he proposes "constructive" or "revisionist" liberalism; in still another, to distinguish his view from the old narrowly economic one, "sociological liberalism." Granville Hicks has deftly employed the phrase "critical liberalism," but this has a literary quality that will hardly do in politics. In a pamphlet which reaches me from Paris,* M. Berger-Perrin calls

---

* "Vitalité Libérale: Physionomie et avenir du Libéralisme renaissant." Editions SEDIF, Paris.

himself a "spiritual liberal" (*libéral-spiritualiste*) adopting a position akin to that of the publishers of *Faith And Freedom* in Los Angeles. It is not logical or wise, however, in gathering recruits for an economic and political order that will permit individual variation in all phases of life, to impose an opinion about other than economic and political topics. Other terms employed by M. Berger-Perrin, "realist liberalism," "humanist liberalism," seem to me also, though in lesser degree, to suffer from this defect.

The term "scientific liberalism," which I find myself employing in conversation with certain sorts of people, is perhaps also subject to this criticism. For me it implies a rejection, not only of the collectivist program, but of the pretense of Marxists that their system of wishful metaphysics is "scientific" as opposed to "utopian" socialism—a hoax that deluded four whole generations of radical idealists. It also conveys, or should convey, the notion of a developing hypothesis rather than a fixed and venerated doctrine. And it states what is certainly true, that man's hopes as a social animal rest in the advancing methods and gradually arriving results of science, not in any new doctrinal obsession or panacea gospel that will start another stampede. However, its technical and laboratorial flavor unfits it for the task we have in mind. To many it would seem, even more than *libéralisme spiritualiste*, to suggest a sect rather than a sensible understanding of things.*

---

* There is considerable reaction these days against what is called "scientism" in the study of man. It means a pretentious imitation in dealing with social problems of the ways and methods of the physical sciences. The term is unfortunate, for science is nothing but the persistent and skilled use of the mind, and the stores of human knowledge, about any problem. If its findings are to be valid, they require in every field the same discipline—the discipline of suspended judgment, elimination of the personal factor, patience in the effort to be consistent, a serene passion for verification. The methodological differences are only those dictated by the subject matter. For that reason, after you have classified certain sociological false pretenses as "scientism," you have to undo the work by proceeding to explain that scientism itself

There are, according to a recent calculation, "some two hundred influential personalities in various countries—economists, sociologists, historians, philosophers of civilization, publicists, and statesmen," who stand for "a renaissance of liberal principles." ** I have not searched their writings through, but it would appear that no single term or convenient phrase has emerged which would distinguish them in popular parlance from Soviet sympathizers or enthusiasts of the New Deal or the British planned economy state.

"True Liberalism," a phrase used by Ludwig von Mises, seems to suggest, although it ought not to, something fixed in the past, to be adhered to rather than developed. And "the New Liberalism," while most natural as an abstract noun, provides no personal designation. A man can not very well call himself a New Liberal—especially since he will probably be old, and so will the New Liberalism, before he gets anywhere near his goal.

Of all the current ways of rebaptizing the world liberal Roepke's term "liberal conservative," once applied to the followers of Robert Peel, seems to me the most adroit. The noun is a frank admission that civilization is on the defensive; to be "progressive" in the direction the world is going is to be wrong. The central effort of the free market economists is to conserve what they perceive to have been the indispensable frame and instrument of our progress in the past. And yet what they are conserving was associated in its earlier phase

---

"is unscientific in the true sense of the word" (Hayek, "Scientism and the Study of Society," *Economica,* February 1944). It would be better to avoid in the first place that extravagant adulation of mathematical physics out of which the whole difficulty arose. As I read their glib and changeful pronouncements about the size, shape and behavior of "the universe," I feel that there is about as much "scientism" among the physicists as among the rest of us.

** Dr. Muller-Armack in the Bulletin of the University of Kiel, 1950, cited by Berger-Perrin in the above-mentioned pamphlet.

with the term liberalism, and its defenders were called liberals. The combination of these two honest words might put up quite a stout resistance, I should think, both to the atrocities of demagogues and the more subtle corruptions practiced upon language by history.

POSTSCRIPT

When this chapter was first published in the *Freeman* magazine in August 1953, the editor suggested that I had failed to consider the term "libertarian." I did consider it and pass it over, not only because it has too long a tail, but because it has been taken up by people having a sort of irresponsibility to the practical terms in which problems present themselves to the race of man. These people have a disposition to lock themselves in a closet with the abstract truth. Or rather, perhaps, they set themselves aloft on a pedestal, issuing pronunciamentos from the standpoint of a supernal rationality rather than an anxious consideration of what it may be possible, things and people being what they are, to do. The hero and archetype of this Smart Aleck School of thought was Albert J. Nock, who designated himself, correctly, I think, and for this reason, "a superfluous man." Wisdom requires, it seems to me, that we regard ourselves as members of the human race, sharing those basic characteristics which give rise to the problems we are attempting to solve. And I have the impression that, by and large, those who call themselves libertarians fail to remember this somewhat humiliating but indubitable truth. They inherit the arrogance and irresponsibility, if not quite the dash and high spirits, of the once formidable anarchists.

My own principal reflection since publishing the essay is that "liberal conservative" has an arm-chairish flavor that is inappropriate to the fight we are in. The term "radical conservative," employed in a recent article by E. Merrill Root, sounds better. And it is more in accord with the suggestions made in this book. The Distributive State as an ultimate ideal, while it would conserve the values already achieved, is as radical as socialism was. A program of more goods and fewer people is far at least from reactionary. And to maintain an equilibrium of conflicting forces, cutting down any one whatever that tends to dominate society, is certainly a radical approach to the defense of freedom. I think "radical conservative" will meet the needs at least of the present situation.

THE RELIGION
OF IMMORALISM

Chapter Seven

SINCE Stalin's death it has become necessary
to find a new focus for our hostility to the unscrupulous and
inhuman behavior of the Communists. I wish it might be
focused on the real cause of the trouble: Marxism. Much
force of argument is wasted among Western intellectuals
through a wish to exempt Marx from responsibility for this return to barbarism. Realpolitik in the evil sense was certainly
not born with Marx. But the peculiar thing we are up against,
the casting aside of moral standards by people specializ-
ing in the quest of ideal human relations, *was* born with
Marx. He is the fountain source of the mores as well as the
economics of the Russian Bolsheviks, and is the godfather of
the delinquent liberals in all lands.

The notion of Marx as a benign and noble brooder over
man's hopes and sorrows, who would be "horrified" at the
tricks and duplicities of present-day Communists, is as false
as it is widespread. Marx had a bad character. His best

81

eulogists can hardly think up a virtue to ascribe to him—except, indeed, tenacity and moral courage. If he ever performed a generous act, it is not to be found in the record. He was a totally undisciplined, vain, slovenly, and egotistical spoiled child. He was ready at the drop of a hat with spiteful hate. He could be devious, disloyal, snobbish, antidemocratic, anti-Semitic, anti-Negro. He was by habit a sponge, an intriguer, a tyrannical bigot who would rather wreck his party than see it succeed under another leader. All these traits are clear in the records of his life, and above all in his private correspondence with his *alter ego* and inexhaustible sugar-daddy, Friedrich Engels. There are bits in this correspondence so revolting to a person of democratic sensibility that they had to be suppressed to keep the myth of the great-hearted Karl Marx, champion of the downtrodden and of human brotherhood, alive at all. To give one example: Ferdinand Lassalle, who was eclipsing Marx as leader of a genuine working class movement in Germany, they discovered to be not only a Jew whom they called "Baron Izzy," "oi-oi, the great Lassalle," "the little Jew," "the little kike," "Jew Braun," "Izzy the bounder," etc., but also "a Jewish nigger." "It is perfectly obvious," Marx wrote, "from the shape of his head and the way his hair grows that he is descended from the Negroes who joined Moses on the journey out of Egypt, unless perhaps his mother or his grandmother had relations with a nigger." Only the Russian Bolsheviks, who went in for the religion of immoralism with a barbaric candor impossible to an urbane European, had the hardihood to publish these letters unexpurgated.

I use the word religion in a precise sense. Although he dismissed God as a hoax and the heavenly paradise as a decoy, Marx was not by nature skeptical or experimental. His habits of thought demanded a belief both in paradise and in a power that would surely lead us to it. He located his paradise on earth, calling it by such beatific names as the "Kingdom of Freedom," the "Society of the Free and Equal," the "Classless Society," etc. Everything would be blissful and harmonious there to a degree surpassing even the dreams of the utopian socialists. Not only would all "causes for contest" disappear, all caste and class divisions, but all divisions between city and country, between brain and manual worker. Men would not even be divided into different professions as they are at this low stage of the climb toward paradise.

"Socialism will abolish both architecture and barrow-pushing as professions," Engels assured the believers, "and the man who has given half an hour to architecture will also push the cart a little until his work as an architect is again in demand. It would be a pretty sort of socialism which perpetuated the business of barrow-pushing."

It would seem that only a benign deity could guarantee such a future to mankind, and only by teaching a higher morality could He lead us to it. But Marx hated deity, and regarded high moral aspirations as an obstacle. The power on which he rested his faith in the coming paradise was the harsh, fierce, bloody evolution of a "material," and yet mysteriously "upward-going," world. And he convinced himself that, in order to get in step with such a world, we must set aside moral principles and go in for fratricidal war. Although buried under a mountain of economic rationalizations pretending to be science, that mystical and antimoral faith is the one wholly original contribution of Karl Marx to man's heritage of ideas.

It is common among those who condemn the lowering of moral standards by Marxists to blame their "materialism" for it, but that is a crass mistake. Throughout history, from Democritus to Santayana, men who believed genuinely that the substance of the world is matter have been among the noblest teachers of morality. Marx's materialism was not genuine. It was the disguise of a mystical faith. The world he called "material" was mental enough to be forever ascending "from the lower to the higher" with a determinism that is hardly distinguishable from determination. Engels, who did the work and took the risk of actually expounding this naive philosophy—for Marx played it safe as well as lazy by only jotting down a few notes—even tells us that "the celestial bodies like the formation of the organisms . . . arise and perish and the courses that they run . . . take on eternally more magnificent dimensions." Remembering that on this particular planet human society is also rising through successive stages to the "more magnificent" goal of the socialist society, you see what a godlike kind of "matter" it was that Marx believed in. It differed from Hegel's Divine Spirit only in agreeing with Marx about what *is* sublime, and in mapping out a course of procedure toward it that gave free exercise to Marx's rebellious and contumaceous disposition. The universe of dialectic materialism—to put it briefly—is a pantheistic God masquerading as matter, and permitting Himself under that disguise forms of conduct that no God honestly named and identified could get away with in a civilized world.

Whittaker Chambers is very profoundly wrong when he says in his book, *Witness,* that the issue between Soviet Communism and the free world is between religion and irreligion, or between belief in man and belief in God. The Communists believe in man not as an independent power, but as a constituent part of the superhumanly ordained movement of the universe. That dialectic movement is their God, and it is that God who exempts them from the laws of morality. The difference between Christianity and Communism—the difference, I mean, that is vital in this connection—is between a religion which teaches personal salvation through sympathy and loving-kindness and a religion which teaches social salvation through bringing the morals of war into the peacetime relations of men.

Marx was so sure that the world was going to be redeemed by its own dialectic evolution that he would not permit his disciples to invoke the guidance of moral ideals. He really meant it when he said the workers have "no ideal to realize," they have only to participate in the contemporary struggle. He expelled people from his Communist party for mentioning programmatically such things as "love," "justice," "humanity," even "morality" itself. "Soulful ravings," "sloppy sentimentality," he called such expressions, and purged the astonished authors as though they had committed the most dastardly crimes.

Later in life, when Marx founded the First International, he felt compelled for the sake of a big membership to soft-pedal his highbrow insight into the purposes of the universe. He wrote privately to Engels: "I was obliged to insert in the preamble two phrases about 'duty and right,' ditto 'truth, morality, and justice.'" But these lamentable phrases—he assured his friend—"are placed in such a way that they can do no harm."

This mystic faith in evolution set Marx's mind free, and, alas, his natural disposition, to replace the honest campaign of public persuasion by which other gospels have been propagated, with schemes for deceiving the public and tricking his way into positions of power. It was Marx, not Lenin, who invented the technique of the "front organization," the device of pretending to be a democrat in order to destroy democracy, the ruthless purging of dissident party members, the employment of false personal slander in this task.

It was Marx and Engels who adopted "scorn and contempt" as the major key in which to attack the opponents of socialism, introducing a literature of vituperation that has few parallels in history. Even the political masterstroke of giving the land to the peasants "initially" in order to take it away from them when the power is secure came from the same source. The introduction of such unprincipled behavior into a movement toward the highest ends of man was entirely the work of Marx and Engels. Lenin added nothing to it but skill, and Stalin nothing but total instinctive indifference to the ends.

So strong a force was set going after his death to sanctify Marx, and *benevolize* him, so to speak, that these practices were largely forgotten among Western Socialists. His religion of immoralism was smoothed over. But in Lenin's mind this religion found a perfect home, for Lenin had grown up under the influence of the terrorist wing of the Russian revolutionary movement. Lenin was an ardent admirer of Nechayev, a rabid zealot of the 1870's who drew up a famous document called "Catechism of a Revolutionist."

"The revolutionist is a doomed man. . . . He has severed every link with the social order and with the entire civilized world. . . . He hates and despises the social morality of his time. . . . Everything which promotes the success of the revolution is moral, everything which hinders it is immoral."

Nechayev was denounced even by his sufficiently violent colleague, the anarchist Bakunin, as a dangerous fanatic, who "when it is necessary to render some service to what he calls 'the cause' . . . stops at nothing—deceit, robbery, even murder." But Lenin startled his early friends by defending this madman and honoring his memory. Thus before he became a Marxist, Lenin had arrived by an emotional road at that rejection of moral standards which Marx deduced from a pretended science of history. The confluence of these two streams of thought is one of the greatest disasters that ever befell mankind.

Lenin was even more credulous and more specific than Marx and Engels in describing the beauties of life in the paradise toward which this dialectic world was traveling. In his socialism every "barrow-pusher" and every kitchen maid was to take part in the function of government. He was also more specific in describing the kinds of vile conduct which must be employed to help it along. "We must be ready to employ trickery, deceit, law-breaking, withholding and concealing truth," he exclaimed. "We can and must write in a language which sows among the masses hate, revulsion, scorn, and the like, toward those who disagree with us."

Acting upon such principles, Lenin made use of slanderous lies and character-assassinations; he encouraged bank robberies and armed holdups as a means of replenishing the funds for the millennium. His disciples have carried the faith forward, not stopping at any crime, from bodily assassination to state-planned famine and wholesale military massacre. A chief organizer of those bank robberies and holdups was the Georgian Djugashvili, who took the party name of Stalin. The Marx-Leninist belief that such crimes are methods of progress toward a millennium was instilled in this youth from the day of his revolt against Christian theology. He had no other education, touched no other conception of the world. He was once described by Archbishop Curley as "the greatest murderer of men in history," and the record when it is calmly written may bear this out. But he took no step beyond the logical implications of a devout belief in brutal and dishonorable conduct. He merely followed through on the doctrine invented by Karl Marx, that in order to enter the "Kingdom of Freedom," we must set aside moral standards. We must place "duty and right . . . truth, morality, and justice," where "they can do no harm." Or, in Lenin's words (spoken to an all-Russian Congress of Youth):

"For us morality is subordinated completely to the interests of the class struggle of the proletariat."

We have not entered, alas, the Kingdom of Freedom, and the Classless Society has failed to appear. Everything under the Communists moves in the opposite direction. But this religion of immoralism flourishes. The notion of an earthly paradise in which men shall dwell together in millennial brotherhood is used to justify crimes and depravities surpassing anything the modern world has seen. And this is true not only in Russia, but wherever the power of the Communist conspiracy extends. In countries beyond the reach of Moscow the taint is carried by Communist parties to their fringe of accomplices, dupes, and fellow travelers; even the once-honest liberals are not immune to it. More and more throughout the world those dedicated to an extreme social ideal, instead of being trained in virtue, are trained to condone crimes against the elementary principles of social conduct. Such a disaster never happened to humanity before. No such religion ever existed. That is why our statesmen have been bewildered and outwitted by it. Even after thirty years of being assiduously swindled by the Kremlin, they find it hard to believe that any human animal can be, on principle and with devout and selfless fervor, a liar, a murderer, and a cheat.

They are now looking for some recrudescence of the old simple decencies in Malenkov and his associates. But they will look in vain. These men have been brought up in the same school. They are fanatics of the same antimoral and antiscientific religion. Only the disproof and dislodgment of Marxism will ever cure the world of its present desperate sickness.

A WORD ABOUT
MARX AND MACHIAVELLI
Chapter Eight

It is customary to describe the new Marxian immoralism, and the devious and vicious conduct of its Soviet apostles, as Machiavellian. But that is a whitewash of Marxism and a slander against Machiavelli that, even in his least elevating counsels, he little deserves. These counsels of duplicity were addressed only to a "Prince," to whom he looked, not for ideal government in general—as to that he was a republican—but for the specific task of unifying the Italian nation in the circumstances of his time. It is one thing to suggest that in dominating a society regulated by aristocratic tradition and the mores of feudal caste, a prince may hold himself immune to moral judgments. It is a very different thing, in trying to pass from political democracy to a more ideally cooperative form of social union, to offer the same immunity to "the proletariat" conceived as the "great majority" of mankind. Machiavellian is not a suitable name for this, because the word suggests serious reflection. An insane act of self-frustration would be a better name for it—

an injection of poison into the lifeblood of the society you are proposing to improve.

It is not sophisticated, but merely frivolous, to deny the political importance of moral character and moral principles. Of course they are important. But this does not require us to become mystical about conscience, or imagine that being good differs at bottom from being intelligent. If the whole causal nexus were known, moral judgments could hardly turn out to be anything more or better than scientific. It happens, however, that in social and political matters there exists no science, no detailed technical knowledge, capable of replacing the principles of common sense. It is utopian to imagine that such a body of knowledge ever will exist. To those who strive only for power, that does not matter. But those who cherish civilization, or want to better it, will restore the judgment of men and their behavior to the position in political enterprise that it holds, and always has held, and always will hold, in practical and personal affairs.

Civilization itself is little but a set of learned attitudes and social habits. Chief among them is the demand men habitually make upon themselves and their associates for mutual respect of dignity, for truthful, kind, sincere, and loyal and honorable conduct. Civilization is on the defensive now. It is fighting for its life. It needs, in order to fight well, a vision of the future, a sense of growth toward better things. It needs a young and courageous vanguard. But let us hope that the young and courageous, the new generation in whom hope always resides, will not mix their projects for the improvement of social life with a contempt for those elementary wisdoms which have made social life possible.

Part Two

Note

The two following chapters, "The Word Socialism" and "Socialism and Human Nature," were originally one essay, and were written with the thought of condensation in the *Reader's Digest*. Writing for the *Reader's Digest*, while not exactly an art, is a highly specialized craft. The magazine is largely concerned with the life of ideas, but as it is addressed to some fifty or sixty million readers—the actual copies printed numbering over seventeen million—the ideas have to be presented with a self-explanatory simplicity. I have learned this craft by thinking of myself as a teacher when writing essays of this kind for the *Reader's Digest*. If the present reader is too learned to be approached in this way, I trust he will be magnanimous. I doubt if it will really do him any harm to run over briefly, while we are discussing the subject, what he already knows about socialism. If the mode of presentation seems a little elementary, the effort was not the less intense. This was the first announcement, written in 1941, of my changed opinion about socialism, and I weighed every word of it.

THE WORD SOCIALISM—
ITS STRANGE
ADVENTURES

Chapter Nine

THE word socialism was born a hundred and eighteen years ago in excited talk about the ideas of Robert Owen, a kindly English gentleman with shy eyes and a mighty nose and a great passion for apple dumplings. Owen came over to America in 1825 and bought a whole town and 30,000 acres of land out in Indiana on the banks of the Wabash. He issued a sweeping invitation to the "industrious and well disposed of all nations" to come out there and join him in the ownership of this property, and start living in co-operative peace and loving-kindness as nature had intended man to live. The place had been called "New Harmony" by a band of German monks who founded it, and that suited Owen's scheme ideally.

Owen was a shrewd and brilliant businessman, a sort of larger-visioned Henry Ford, and America welcomed him with her most royal gift of publicity. The Hall of Congress in Washington was turned over to him, and he explained socialism—and showed pictures of it—to an audience containing, among others, the President of the United States, a majority of both Houses of Congress, and most of the Justices of the Supreme Court.

"I am come to this country," he announced, "to introduce an entire new state of society, to change it from an ignorant, selfish system to an enlightened, social system which shall gradually unite all interests into one, and remove all causes for contest between individuals."

In France the word *socialisme* had a slightly different origin, but not very different. Owen's effort to attain beatitude in Indiana was repeated forty-one times in other parts of the long-suffering United States by followers of the French apostle of harmony, Fourier.* As they all had like results, we may take Owen's little ramshackle paradise on the banks of the Wabash as typical of these recklessly noble attempts, by combining love with rationality, to bring heaven down to earth. It perfectly represents the meaning of the word socialism at its birth.

And it held together only so long as Robert Owen stayed there and bossed it. Left to themselves, its thousand-odd members fell to chiseling and snitching and indulging in rather more slander, if you can imagine it, than is usual. After two years they "divvied" up in a cool mood and quit. Owen thought it was because "the habits of the individual system" prevailing in the rest of the world were too strong.

Nothwithstanding this dismal and swift failure, Owen's idea—that if *business* were run on cooperative principles, life in general would become friendly and harmonious—grad-

---

* St. Simon is generally mentioned with Fourier and Owen as one of the fathers of utopian socialism, but his utopia was of so different a kind from theirs that its character was distorted somewhat by the very application of the name. See in this connection "Les Deux Socialismes" by Robert Louzon in *La Révolution Prolétarienne* for March and April 1948.

ually became the dominant one among radical minds the world over. It gave birth through the years to a whole litter of differently shaded ideas: syndicalist, communist, guild-socialist, social-revolutionary, bolshevik, menshevik, Fabian socialist, Christian socialist, I.W.W., anarchist, etc. They differed as to how the new harmony was to be achieved, but they did not differ importantly about Robert Owen's fundamental general idea. For over a hundred years, even by many who could not subscribe to it as a practical measure, that idea, baptized with the name of socialism, was assumed to represent the highest hopes of civilization.

Three really big things happened to the socialist idea in the course of these hundred-odd years. Around the middle of the past century, a cocksure, angry, and pedantic genius by the name of Karl Marx undertook to prove that, although it had failed so dismally in Indiana, it was *inevitably coming true* throughout the world. Marx was personally more impractical than Owen. He was as far away as you can get from a successful businessman. He floundered in dire financial straits most of his life long, and hardly ever managed to finish anything he undertook to do. He was not troubled with loving-kindness, either—not at all the type to usher in millenniums on a retail plan by personal example. But Marx had a brain like a high-powered locomotive engine, and when he set out to prove a thing, there was nothing for ordinary facts or practical considerations to do but get out of the way. Marx made his proof so comprehensive and so cloudy, and wound up so much true science with the romantic metaphysics out of which it was concocted, that he actually convinced the best radical minds of three generations that Robert Owen's dream *was* inevitably coming true.

It was not coming true because some more benign Englishmen were going to subsidize some more credulous Americans and demonstrate how noble it was. It was coming true, noble or not, because the whole of present-day society was going to split violently in half like a growing acorn. In irresistible revolutionary struggle the under and larger half, those without property, were going to grab the land and industries and *impose* this dream on the upper half by state force. No more postcard utopias on the banks of the Wabash! No more trust in the "well disposed"! Hard-headed, hard-fisted proletarians were going to put the thing across. The owners of the world, hopelessly "bourgeois," didn't *want* a New Harmony—that's why Robert Owen failed. Well, they were going to get a New Harmony whether they wanted one or not. And they were going to get it—to translate the Marxian state of feeling very exactly—"in the neck."

That was the first big thing that happened to the word socialism. From meaning a practical experiment it came to mean a metaphysical certainty, and from a vessel of brotherly emotion it turned into the battle-cry of a class fight. It became the "war aim" of the workers in their impending inevitable robber raid against the whole capitalist class.

The second big thing that happened—and life was seventy more years getting this ready—was that such a raid did actually occur. It occurred in Russia, the last place where anybody was looking for it, and it occurred largely because a great political genius gave his heart to Owen's dream and his mind to Marx's metaphysics.

Lenin was personally more like Robert Owen than like Karl Marx. He combined the same grandiose idealism with the same canny gift for getting things done. He had no special zeal for apple dumplings, but he had a similarly homelike love for cats. He had a hearty affection for people, too, that was notably lacking in Marx. He looked like an able executive who had lost his hair, though none of his vigor, sitting at a desk bossing a big industry. He *was* an able executive, and could have bossed a big industry. As head of the

"Community of Equality" at New Harmony he would have made, while he lasted, a thriving success.

But Lenin's role in history was totally shaped and determined by the writings of Karl Marx. He believed fanatically—if that means absolutely and to the last detail—in the whole Marxian system. In his penciled comments on the margins of the Marxian texts he studied, there is not one word of dissent or disagreement. He learned Marx like a schoolboy, slavishly and with adoration. And yet in practice he was independent, alert, flexible, cunning, alive to new developments—possessed of a native intelligence superior, in my opinion, to that of his master.

In the name of socialism Lenin took charge of an actual revolution, led it to victory, and set going on the scale of the Russian empire the same romantic experiment that Robert Owen failed with on the banks of the Wabash ninety years before.

And the results were not better than Robert Owen's but a million times worse. In his speeches before he seized power, Lenin promised the same wonderful things, and even more wonderful than Owen had promised at New Harmony:

"Democracy from below!" he shouted. "Democracy without an officialdom, without police, without a standing army . . . Immediate preparation for a state of things where *all* shall fulfill the functions of control and superintendence, so that none shall have the opportunity of becoming bureaucrats at all. . . . The state itself will wither away, by virtue of the simple fact that, freed from capitalist slavery, from the innumerable horrors, savagery, absurdities and infamies of capitalist exploitation, people will gradually *become accustomed* to the observation of the elementary rules of social life, known for centuries, repeated for thousands of years in all sermons. They will become accustomed to their observance without constraint, without subjection, without the special apparatus for compulsion which is called the State!"

That is the New Harmony Lenin promised, and the result is now well known: Officialdom gone mad, officialdom erected into a new and merciless exploiting class; the largest peace-time standing army in the world; the people universally *disarmed;* the functions of control and superintendence gripped in the fist of a ruling clique which, when needful, wages armed war on the people; the "slavery . . . horrors, savagery, absurdities and infamies of capitalist exploitation" so far outdone that they are talked of in secret as a lost paradise; bureaucrats everywhere, and behind the bureaucrats a gigantic army of high-paid state police; death for those who question or protest, death by execution without trial or by state-planned starvation in a slave camp.

There are, strangely enough, specimens of the human brain whose owners still insist that this is a New Harmony in the making. Knaves, many of them, who have a job or prestige requiring that they say so; mental cowards, others, who, having put their faith in Lenin's Marxism, lack the pluck to live without that faith. To honest men with courage to confront facts it is clear that Lenin's experiment, like Robert Owen's, failed.

It failed, however, in a different way. It did not drop naturally apart because the boss went home and let it run itself as it was supposed to. The boss, alas, stayed all too firmly on the job. It failed because it was *prevented* by military force from dropping naturally apart—by bayonets, machine guns, spies, chain-gangs, concentration camps, murder, massacre, and engineered starvation. It failed as a libertarian and humane hope because as a going concern it survived. It survived long enough to show what was in it: tyranny, namely, and that new perfection of tyranny, the totalitarian state. That new bloody thing wears, on all the maps of the world, the name of "socialist."

Such is the main road traveled in a hundred and fifty

years by the word socialism. It wandered down a branch road during the nineteenth century, and arrived on the emblems of another bloody police state—National Socialist Germany. It seems to know better than its creators and gentle-minded proprietors where it belongs. They will have trouble erasing it, anyway, from the histories of this whole epoch, the maps of the earth, the banners of the armies of fourteen nations. Might it not be better, instead of clinging to the word socialism, trying with mere adjectives to drag it back in the direction of its origins, to find out, if we can, what the basic mistake was of those who started it off on this strange and dreadful adventure?

SOCIALISM AND HUMAN NATURE

Chapter Ten

W<small>HY</small> did the benign dream of Fourier and Owen, when made plausible by the rationalizations of Marx, and dynamic by the engineering genius of Lenin, turn into a nightmare? I think the reason, if you go to the depth of it, is single and very simple. It is because these men and all their tens of millions of followers, notwithstanding their bold scorn of superstition and firm determination to be realistic, had a naive and romantic conception of what a man is.

Both the utopians and Karl Marx did their thinking before psychology as we know it, or anthropology, or even biology in its modern form, was born. And Lenin, as I said, did no theoretic thinking that passed beyond Karl Marx. Lenin was only twenty years old when William James published his epoch-making *Psychology,* but there is not a sign in his writing that he ever read so much as the title of an elementary textbook in this developing science.

In October 1917, after the news came that Kerensky's

government had fled, and the Winter Palace had fallen to his insurrectionary troops, Lenin, who had been in hiding, appeared at a meeting of the Workers' and Soldiers' Soviet of Petrograd. He walked rapidly up the aisle, mounted the rostrum, and when the long, wild, happy shouts of greeting had died down, remarked:

"We will now proceed to the construction of a socialist society."

He said this as simply as though he were proposing to put up a new barn for the cows or a modern hen house. But in all his life he had never asked himself the equally simple question:

"How is this ingenious invention going to fit with the instinctive tendencies of the animals it is made for?"

The idea had never entered Lenin's head that men, like other animals, might *have* instinctive tendencies. He actually knew less about this subject, after a hundred years, than Robert Owen did. Owen had described human nature fairly well for an amateur as "a compound of animal propensities, intellectual faculties and moral qualities." He had written into the preamble of the Constitution of New Harmony that "Man's character . . . is the result of his formation, his location, and of the circumstances within which he exists." He merely omitted to think about that factor of man's "formation"—what we call his hereditary nature—until his wish had time to convince him that "location" and "circumstance" could do everything. Plant people in a cooperative society young enough, he persuaded himself, and they will grow up just, reasonable, truthful, magnanimous—they will grow up *cooperative*.

To say nothing of science, it would seem a mere matter of common sense, if you wanted to improve upon Owen's system, to go down into the details and find out something a little more exact and reliable about "man's character." If the

thing had happened in England or France, that would probably have been the next step. But it happened in Germany,
and the natural procedure was to fly up out of the details
into the empyrean. Instead of a more circumspect plan for
progress, we got a system of philosophy in which progress
was incidental. Marx *deduced* socialism from a theory of
the universe which he had learned at school, and which happened to be fashionable at the moment. For this reason,
with all the great talk about advancing from "utopian" to
"scientific," Marx took a long step backward from Robert
Owen's comparatively sensible approach to his problem. He
dropped out "formation" or "propensity"—the problem of
man's hereditary nature—altogether. He dropped out man
altogether, so far as he might present an obstacle to social
change.

"Man," he said, "is a complex of social relations . . . The
individual has no real existence outside the milieu in which
he lives." By which he meant: *Change the social relations,
change the milieu, and man will change as much as you like.*
"All history," he added, "is nothing but a continual transformation of human nature."

That is all Marx ever said on this primary, and in a scientific mind, preliminary, question. And Lenin, I repeat,
said nothing. That is why their dream turned into a nightmare. That is the rock-bottom reason. Their scheme was amateur—and worse than amateur, mystical—on the very subject most essential to its success.

To be sure, we cannot jump in with a pretense that we
know much about the subject even now. The science of human behavior is still in its infancy. Biology, anthropology,
sociology, psychology—they have hardly even joined forces
yet, or agreed upon a common language. They have, however, a valid mode of approach and certain concepts to

which any man seriously concerned with social change must give attention. As a studious reader of these sciences, I will venture to mention four or five of these concepts, which I think largely explain why, instead of the New Harmony he expected, Lenin produced the horrors of a totalitarian state.

It is not that men are greedy or acquisitive merely. Both men and women, and especially the youth, were sacrificial of this world's goods in both Lenin's Russia and Hitler's Germany to the point of sainthood and in droves. Those wiseacres who used to growl about the greediness of men, and say on that ground, "You socialists don't know anything about human nature!" really didn't know very much more than we did. It wouldn't have hurt either of us to study the subject.

Man is, to begin with, the most plastic and adaptable of animals. He truly can be changed by his environment, and even by himself, to a unique degree, and that makes extreme ideas of progress reasonable. On the other hand he inherits, besides "animal propensities" in the crude sense, a set of emotional drives or impulses—the word instinct is a risky one —which, although they can be trained in various ways in the individual, cannot be eradicated from the race. Training consists only of repressing or redirecting them. And no matter how much they may be altered by the "location and circumstance" of the parent, they reappear in the original form—as sure as the hedgehog puts out spines—in every baby that is born.

This native endowment, moreover, was evolved in prehistoric times. In general it fitted man, or those men at least from whom we are descended, for survival in savage tribes. Nothing has happened in the brief span of racial life called "civilized" to alter measurably what we are at birth. The learned attitudes and modes of behavior which, together with manufactured objects, constitute civilization, are not transmitted in heredity, and have to be acquired anew by every individual.

This much about human nature can, I think, be properly described as knowledge. When it comes to stating just what those native tendencies are, however, differences of opinion arise that make the going difficult. Freud solved the problem, or concealed it, by lumping them all together and calling them id. As Freud is always stressing the central importance of sex, and as id is the Latin word for "it," this academic device had a very unacademic appropriateness when it arrived on our slangy shores. But it did not blind judicious eyes to the irreducible variety of drives in man's hereditary nature.

One of them upon which even Freud agrees is an aggressive or pugnacious tendency. It seems that whenever this human animal is frustrated in any of his impulses, he is likely to get an impulse to lambaste somebody. And as all of us in the nature of things are a good part frustrated all the time, there is always a plenty of pugnacity lying round. As a carefully scientific book says: "One may think of each nation as having a large number of individuals who are constantly in need of some person, some idea, or some group toward whom aggression may be expressed." * This, I think, is what made Marx's doctrine so much more popular than Fourier's or Owen's. The three men talked about the same ultimate goal of peace and harmony on earth. But Marx talked very little about it, and meanwhile gave his followers a chance to fight. To *arrive* at the goal they must forswear peace and harmony and go in for a battle of the ages.

A wiser scheme would preserve some of that belligerent

---

* *Frustration and Aggression*, Dollard, Doob, Miller, Mowrer and Sears. (Yale Institute of Human Relations.)

excitement in its future goal. It would fashion an ideal a little less like heaven than the "classless society," a little more like having fun on earth. "From each according to his abilities, to each according to his needs," sounds very just and noble, but if you use your imagination a little:—What a bore it would be!

"At least let's take time out every afternoon," the too-blessed citizens would say, "and see what each can grab."

I hope I do not sound frivolous, for I am saying the most important thing I know how to say about socialism. It has been more myth than science. Its aim has been escape from reality rather than adjustment to it. Instead of trying to "remove all causes for contest between individuals," as Owen did, or even between classes, as Marx did, we ought to recognize that contest forms a large part of what keeps mankind in health and interested. Progress must consist in elevating the level and humanizing the terms on which the vital contests are fought. This takes perhaps a little of the flame out of the heart of the revolutionist, but it will keep a light shining in his head. If it is true, or anywhere near true, as Marx said, that "All history is a history of class struggles," then the attempt at a classless society is an attempt to jump out of history. The Bolsheviks did indeed jump out of history, or jump into this form of tyranny which history had never seen before. The task is to guide history, using above all things our knowledge of man to make his future more satisfying to his instinctive nature.

That is the most obvious thing, I think, that psychology has to say to the socialist. The ideal society must be adapted to the unideal man. It must have regard to native average human traits, and not confuse these with subtle attitudes that specially bred or educated types have sometimes managed to maintain. And among these traits a gift for giving battle will be found quite as native as that gregarious kindliness of which socialists have made so much.

Another trait of man that socialism has ignored—and indeed all political idealisms from Plato's *Republic* to the Declaration of Independence—is involved in that gregarious or social drive itself. It is not a simple disposition to stand side by side, or chat together, or do together what has to be done. It is a disposition enabling a number of distinct and wayward individuals to cohere when necessary and act as a unit. To this end each individual has to be capable of adopting toward his neighbor, and adopting with impetuous sincerity, an attitude either of dominance or submission. It is this confusing and yet neat pair of attributes that socialists most fatally ignored. Particularly the submissive side has been ignored—the passion both men and women have for being led, for obeying, and conforming, and belonging-to.

Freud sees this tendency in adults as the child in them still yearning for a parent's authority. Others have called it an "instinct of submission," as opposed to an "instinct of self-assertion." Still others have been content to describe the whole thing—and almost everything else besides—as "herd instinct." But that suggests a rather timorous grass-eating herd. "A tendency to fight in packs," might be more appropriate to the present picture of mankind, if you are bound to find first cousins in the zoo. But I do not think that is necessary. We shall get into desperate trouble if we adopt the clichés of any particular school or line of study in psychology. Naturally, if you approach the delineation of man's nature by way of the animals, you will come out with one terminology; if you approach it through primitive communities, you will come out with another; if you approach it through the insane asylum, you will come out with a third. If you approach it with an awe-stricken respect for the methods of mathematical physics you will come out nowhere at all. But I think any authority on the subject, whichever language he might use, would agree that men have in their hereditary nature a good-sized dose of belligerence, and they have a disposition both toward dominating others and submitting to them, which is not an acquired taste. Their appreciation of independence and equality of status, as well as their cooperativeness, is thus qualified by very strong drives of a contrary kind. Is it too much to ask of the architects of a New Society that they take these facts into consideration?

Owen's experiments did not fail, nor Lenin's either, because of the "habits of the individual system" prevailing in its members. It failed, rather, because of the impulses of the social animal prevailing in them. The idea of producing a "Community of Equality"—or in Marx's term, a "Society of the Free and Equal"—by socializing property and production, assumed a greater self-dependence, as well as a more peaceable disposition, than these human animals are born with or capable in large numbers of acquiring. Cats might form such a society if they could learn to work together, but dogs would have to learn to stand on their own feet! And so would all gregarious animals, including even this very teachable and thoughtful one called man.

If these things are true, it is no accident that Owen's community—and the others like it—throve only so long as the founder stayed on hand to boss it. It is no accident that "complete collectivization" in Russia, instead of setting the workers and peasants free, imposed over them a new kind of tyrant. It seems obvious to me now—though I was slow, I must say, in coming to the conclusion—that the institution of private property, the dispersion of power and importance that goes with it, has been a main factor in producing that limited amount of free-and-equalness which Marx hoped to render infinite by abolishing this institution. Marx himself, as

I remarked in another connection,* was the first to realize this. It was he who informed us that the evolution of private capitalism with its free market had been a precondition for the evolution of all our democratic freedoms. It never occurred to him that, if this was so, those other freedoms might disappear with the abolition of the free market.

That, however, is exactly what happened in Russia, and it happened with astounding speed. I do not believe the much over-worked "backwardness" of the country goes one step toward explaining this. Russia's backwardness can hardly explain why collectivization made her more backward. Nor do I believe that the "capitalist encirclement"—so much like Owen's excuse—explains it. Nor even the dictatorial and violent procedures of Lenin's Bolshevik party. It cannot be explained without a reference to those more recently discriminated facts which Marxists out of loyalty to their antique doctrine refuse to think about: the hereditary as against the acquired nature of man; the fact that the hereditary nature is still that of the tribal savage; and that it contains, among other things, a taste for fighting and that tendency to bow down to others or boss them which makes group solidarity in gregarious animals spontaneous.

Particularly in time of stress and danger, men are prone by nature, not just persuadable by argument, to get together and fight. And in that fighting union, all those "moral qualities," the reasonableness and justice, candor and magnanimity, which Owen counted on, and Marx and Lenin after him, tend to give way before those deeper-lying traits. Even calculating self-interest tends to give way. You can not count on anything but cohesion and intolerance.

This, at least, was the exact manner in which the Russian failure came about. The very party of consecrated revolu-

* Chapter II, page 33.

tionists upon whom Lenin had relied to socialize the industries and bring the free society to birth in Russia, became the nucleus of a blind and vengeful fighting gang, stamping to death with shrill yells of hate every individual who dared stand out for Lenin's promises, or for any other thing but anger and obedience.

That is what happened to Lenin's experiment, and began to happen even before his controlling hand was withdrawn. Instead of producing the higher civilization demanded by his amateur science, or no-science, of man, the turmoil of it swept away whole sections of the acquired fabric of civilization altogether, and left the technique of modern industry and education at the mercy of the naked passions of a savage tribe . . .

But let us not malign savage tribes. Within their patterns they cultivate wisdom; they are in a state of growth. It is civilized beings who revert to savagery that are indefensible. Primitive art has its dignity of aspiration, but the cult resulting from the modern imitation of it is already at a dead end. And the same holds of these political and moral retroversions, the totalitarian states, of which that aesthetic cult has been, it almost seems, an anticipation. They are a renunciation of intelligence and of all defined and finely chosen values.

They are a renunciation of everything that Socialists, in particular, set out to multiply. And therefore it is an ironical and sad reflection that the one argument for common ownership that Socialists did base upon the facts of human nature was the argument from savage tribes. "Primitive communism," we used to say, proves that such an economic system is suitable to human nature and will work. It did not occur to us, although it would have been a very "Marxian" occurrence if it had, that in reverting to the economics of savagery, we might revert to its crude level of life. That again, however, is what happened in Russia. There are no better words in which to describe the cultural effect and moral atmosphere of "complete collectivization."

I do not pretend to have given a "scientific explanation" of this complex disaster. It will satisfy me if I have escaped the charge of literary psychology, and convinced the reader that the disaster cannot be explained *without* a science of human nature. It cannot be explained in the old catchwords of economics and class policy. The backers of Hitler in Germany made the same mistake about the Nazi party that the workers and soldiers in Petrograd made about the Bolshevik party. Each group believed that this new brutal, rabid, monolithic fighting gang, on achieving power, would promote, as had been promised, its enlightened interests. Each found that in the growth and triumph of the gang enlightened interest as such disappeared. The gang itself, the perpetuation of its blind fighting power, became the essential goal of the procedure.

Totalitarianism is thus literally an abandonment of civilization itself. And no one who has lived a thinking life these thirty-five years will deny that Lenin's experiment in socialism broke the dam and dug the political channels in which the whole flood is running. It is not enough to pick flaws in the tactics of Lenin; his basic understanding must be questioned. An honest, bold, loyal, and within its limits extremely highbrow attempt to produce through common ownership a society of the Free and Equal, produced a tyrant and a totalitarian state; there sprang up in its wake, borrowing its name and imitating its political procedures, other tyrants and totalitarian states; the whole world was plunged into a brutishly stupid war. I think any wise Socialist, viewing this sequence in the light of what we know and Lenin did not know about human nature, little though it may be, will be inclined to reconsider his assumptions. In his further efforts toward a world in which science shall have conquered poverty and superstition, and made a rich life possible to all, he will be cautious about the scheme of common ownership and state control. He will be cautious about the *extent* to which it may be carried. The more "radical" he is, in the sense of intelligently caring about liberty and justice and a chance at life for the wage workers, the more cautious he will be. Of that I am firmly convinced. Socialism was amateur; we must learn to be expert.

DON'T KILL
THE GOOSE

An Address to the Annual Convention of the
American Federation of Labor, Cincinnati, Ohio,
November 18, 1948

Chapter Eleven

I FEEL a little embarrassed to appear as a re-
spected guest of the American Federation of Labor. In my
palmy days as a revolutionary Socialist, I used to lie awake
nights thinking up ways to insult this organization, denounc-
ing it as the main obstacle on the broad highway to the cooperative commonwealth. My first editorial article, when we
started the old *Masses* in 1912, was an account of the A.F.L.
convention in Rochester, New York. That was the first one,
I think, where the advocates of industrial unionism—led by
Joe Cannon of the Western Federation of Miners, Max Hays
of the Printers Union, and a few others—tried to get up a
revolt against Sam Gompers. I, of course, was all for the revolt, but I wasn't too respectful either of the rebels or the
Gompers machine. "Raisin' Hell in School" was the title of
my article, and just for old times' sake I'll read you a couple
of sentences from it:

"When one of Gompers' men intimated that Johnnie

Walker, a leader of the revolt, was 'advocating free love and
Fletcherism,' and Johnnie got up and started for him, Gompers screamed out: 'Return to your seat at once!' shaking his
gavel at the culprit, for all the world like an irate schoolma'am with a ruler. He had a schoolma'am's manner, too,
when the delegates finished reciting their lessons, of telling
them whether they were right or wrong. He had the same
disposition to sacrifice the true aims of the institution"—by
that I meant the proletarian revolution—"to the necessity of
maintaining discipline. Gompers got to waving his arms
around in his excitement, and finally planted his fist square
in the middle of the water-pitcher, giving everyone on the
platform a liberal shower-bath. That put an end, for the time
being, to the movement for industrial unionism."

Those were great days when the dream of universal freedom under a state-owned economy was still in the sky, when
the down-to-earth experiment was still untried. I am not
ashamed of my loyalty to that dream. Still less am I ashamed
of the fact that when the experiment was tried, and instead
of producing universal freedom, produced the most perfect
tyranny in all history, I was still young enough, or honest
enough—whatever it takes—to say so. Of that I am very
proud.

And I haven't any qualms about giving you exactly the
opposite advice from what I tried unsuccessfully to give Sam
Gompers late one evening in the lobby of a little old hotel in
Rochester thirty-six years ago. My advice is: *Don't kill the
goose that lays the golden eggs.* Capitalism is something of
a goose from the standpoint of abstract reason and the ideal
of perfection. It's easy to make game of that goose, and it's a
lot of fun when you stay up in the sky. But she's the only
creature on this earth that ever laid golden eggs, and in my

humble but mature opinion she's the only one that ever will. My advice to organized labor is: Grab all the eggs you can get your hands on—of course—but watch out. Don't kill the goose!

However, I didn't come here to give advice to organized labor. For one thing, you're not just organized labor any longer. You're a great national power. I suppose you are, especially since the last election, the most powerful private organization in the United States. Together with that power I think you've got to assume a larger responsibility. You've got to think less about the special interests of labor, and more about the problems of our national life as a whole. And our national life is so bound up in the complex of world politics that that means the world as a whole . . .

In the second place, you didn't invite me to this convention as an individual. It is only as a contributing editor of the *New Leader* that I came in for this honor at all. A contributing editor, as you know, is a man who never edits, and keeps the editors in a state of nervous prostration trying to get him to contribute. This puts me in a position to tell you, as the real editors could not, what a wonderful and really heroic institution the *New Leader* is. Without any profit, financial or political, without any recompense whatever but the sense of a great duty well done, the *New Leader* has waged a twenty-five year war against communist infiltration in the labor movement. I don't know any other publication, and hardly another person, except maybe Bill Green and Matt Woll, Dubinsky, George Meany, and a few other of your peculiarly pig-headed officers, who has stood up as long and as resolutely against this insidious form of destruction. It has been a hard, and most of the time a lonely struggle.

It's not so lonely any longer. The people who can't see now that the Communists insert themselves into labor's bat-

tle only to win the power to enslave labor, and all the rest of
mankind, to a new exploiting class are getting fewer and
fewer. Indeed I'm not sure there there is anybody left who
can't see this when he opens his eyes. I don't like to think
that even Henry Wallace is so dumb he doesn't know where
he's heading. You remember that mule the farmer sold at
a very low price, a good, healthy, upstanding, athletic mule,
but when the buyer turned to drive away, the mule ran
straight into a tree.

"Looka here," he yelled, "this mule you sold me is blind!"

"Naw, he ain't blind," the farmer said, "he just don't give
a damn!"

That's how I try to make intelligible to my mind the mental operations of a man like Henry Wallace.

Well, Wallace is out of our way now—at least for the time
being. But that doesn't solve our problem. The fellow travelers are not the immediate difficulty. They are a danger for
the future, but they are not what has got us into this planetary mess, and they are not what is keeping us there.

Ignorance at Washington—and what is more, voluntary ignorance—is the cause of that. They didn't know—they didn't
want to know—what lay behind Stalin's sudden anxiety about
democracy. They didn't want to know the real meaning of the
so-called "dissolution of the Comintern," or the pro-capitalist
twist in the American Communist party line. They didn't
want to know that Stalin made his pact with Hitler in full
knowledge that a war was to follow—a fact recently revealed
to the world by the State Department, but which we in the
New Leader had been shouting from the housetops since long
before the war began. They didn't want to know that the Chinese Communists were hand-in-glove with Stalin in his plan
to seize Manchuria, and then all China, and then all Asia,
and then the world, for the totalitarian revolution. In spite
of our documented revelations of the inside facts in this mat-

ter, they swallowed hook-line-and-sinker the transparent
hoax that the Chinese Communists were some kind of
middle-of-the-road agrarian liberals, who had no connection whatever with the Comintern.

The government's whole Far Eastern foreign policy has
been based on that Moscow-manufactured hoax. I'm not sure
the truth has sunk into General Marshall's mind yet,
although last week Mao Tse-tung himself, the leader of the
Chinese Communists, proclaimed in an international broadcast his absolute solidarity with Stalin in the "world revolutionary united front headed by the Soviet Union." Now that
Manchuria is safe in his hands, and the hoax no longer
needed, this faithful emissary of the Gangster-God in the
Kremlin spits on Secretary Marshall, spits on Edgar Snow
of the *Saturday Evening Post,* spits on Vera Micheles Dean
of the Foreign Policy Association, spits on Owen Lattimore
and the Institute of Pacific Relations, by shouting to the
whole world that the idea of any "middle road" or "third
road" between communism and capitalism is "utter hypoc-
risy and total bankruptcy."

All this was understood and explained in the *New Leader*
with irrefutable documentation week by week throughout
the war. My article, "The Fate of the World Is at Stake in
China," was also published in the *Reader's Digest,* and that
over three years ago. But nobody at Washington paid any
attention to us, except to denounce us as Red Baiters, Em-
bittered Radicals, or people assumed to be spending their
nights and days in the childish pursuit of hating Joe Stalin.
Ignorance at Washington. They didn't know and they
didn't want to know. They wanted to kid themselves. They
wanted to be duped. And one of the master dupesters of all
time was sitting in the Kremlin grinning at the way they
fell for his tricks. He's sitting there now, pulling a big fracas
in Berlin in order to distract their minds while he consoli-

dates his hold on Manchuria and builds his own impregnable Ruhr in the Far East. The plain truth is that, in setting out to wage a planetary war in defense of democratic civilization against the advancing epidemic of totalitarian police states, our statesmen lacked the mental force, or force of character, to face the known facts which would have made it possible to attain the objective for which the war was fought.

I am not talking about the Democratic administration here. I am not sighing over the disappointed hopes of Thomas E. Dewey, or any other Republican. I wish I were. I wish there were any one American leader, Republican or Democrat, who had possessed the penetration and moral courage to talk truth all through this period of self-deception as a world policy. No, the Republicans have been just as ignorant, and more reprehensible, for they were the opposition. It was their natural function to study up and expose the substitution of Sunday School sentimentalism for informed diplomacy which has brought us up to the edge of another war. Instead, they joined in the hymn singing. They chimed with the Democrats in what has been mistakenly called a bipartisan foreign policy. It was a bipartisan no-foreign policy. That is what this country and the world it tried to save has suffered from, and still is suffering from—a non-partisan no-foreign policy. In all that concerns the Soviet Union the sole plan was to express soft sentiments and hide our minds from hard facts. Now we have abandoned the soft sentiments, but we haven't yet faced the hard facts . . .

I propose that we draw a big breath right now and face the essential facts on which an American foreign policy ought to be based. There are only three of them. It's very simple once you get your courage up.

First: Stalin's totalitarian police state is not an approximation to, or something like, or in some respects comparable with Hitler's. It is the same thing, only *more* ruthless, *more* cold-blooded, *more* astute, *more* extreme in its economic policies, *more* explicitly committed to world conquest, and *more* dangerous to democracy and civilized morals.

There are no mitigations of this fact. The Communists pretend that labor occupies some peculiar and privileged position under the Soviet dictatorship. Hitler abolished the trade unions, they say, Stalin preserved them. Stalin did not have to abolish the unions because he had them sewed up in a bag, with all the strings in his hands. That is what I mean by saying that his tyranny is more astute than Hitler's was. This process of boring from within, this attempt of the Communists to get control of the unions by placing disciplined party members in key positions, which you, thank God, are vigorously resisting today, isn't merely a propaganda maneuver. It isn't merely a capture of strategic positions for the insurrectionary seizure of power. It is the laying down of the foundations of the totalitarian state. Once the power is seized, and the party becomes the state, if this infiltration process has been completed, the trade union movement is paralyzed absolutely. Labor becomes an abject and impotent tool in the hands of the state, and of the new exploiting bureaucracy that runs the state.

The fate of the unions in Russia is far worse than destruction. They are flourishing, and their whole strength is dedicated to the opposite aim from that which they were created to serve—the total subjection and absolutely unresisted exploitation of labor. We know from statistics that wages are lower, and the worker's life poorer in Russia than anywhere else in the modern world. But few realize that this political trick of party control by infiltration in the unions is the cause of it. In Russia all the unions are company unions, and the company is the state. It is not only impossible to strike, it is impossible to wiggle a finger of protest against the state-

regulated hours, wages, and conditions of labor. The state
is not only the employer—it is employer, strike-breaker,
private detective and public police force all rolled up in
one.

Another way they have of kidding you that there's a millennium behind the Iron Curtain is to say there's no unemployment under the state-owned economy. There's no "army
of the unemployed" to keep wages down. We don't know
how much unemployment there is in the Soviet Union, but
we know that wages are kept down by an army of slaves
that makes unemployment look like a Sunday School picnic.
The worst fact in modern history, strangely enough, is the
least talked of: the reintroduction into the civilized world of
human slavery in its most cruel and brutal form. Hitler at-
tempted this on the ancient Roman plan, enslaving aliens, or
supposedly "inferior races." He failed because the inferior
races defeated him in war. But Stalin, who does not believe
in racial inequality, has enslaved his own fellow citizens on
a scale not seen before since the world began.

There are, according to the most conscientious estimates,
fourteen millon slaves in GULAG, the slave empire ruled by
the Soviet State Police. That is more than the total population of New York State, including Manhattan. It is more
than the total number of unenslaved industrial workers in
the Soviet Union itself. Which means that the whole so-called
socialist economy rests down on the institution of human
slavery.

These slaves live in corrals surrounded by stockades
topped with barbed wire, watched day and night by
machine-gun men in turrets with powerful searchlights and
packs of ferocious dogs to pursue the runaways. They do the
heaviest, toughest, most grueling and freezing labor, men
and women alike: lumbering, mining, forest clearing, road,
railroad, canal, airdrome and factory construction. One of

their major industries is building additional corrals and barracks for new slaves.

Their labor power is cheap, constant, controllable, "indifferent" (as they say) to climate. It can be transported in freight cars in immense unresisting droves like cattle. It can be used up without worry over capital invested. For these Soviet slaves cost nothing to their owner, the MVD, whose agents simply pick them up on the street, or drag them out of their beds at night.

This cheap labor has become so essential a factor in the economy of the Soviet state that, when the supply runs low, the MVD has been known to issue to each of its local branches a quota of people to be arrested as "socially dangerous elements." For that is the rubric under which the job is done. *Sozialno opassniye elemyenti*—that's all they have to call you.

Doesn't this make a mockery of the pretense that state ownership has solved any real problem—least of all the problem of unemployment? There are more *permanently enslaved* workers in the Soviet Union than there were *temporarily* unemployed workers in the United States during the most desperate years of the depression. It is to hide these facts that the Iron Curtain was pulled down in 1935, and it will stay down as long as there are eyes of free men left in the world to see what monstrous thing has befallen mankind in the name of socialism.

That is the state of things in Russia. That is the first fact which every political leader, and every leader of opinion in the United States is, to my thinking, in honor bound to know, and to confront clearly and bravely, before he utters a peep about world politics, or about any great public question.

The second fact is that the heads of this slave-driving police state are fanatically determined to seize power throughout the world and make over all human society in the image of their state. More exactly, they believe that history is going to accomplish this change, and they are the agents chosen by the historic process to carry it through. There is not, and never has been the slightest doubt about this fact. And yet for three years after the war our statesmen continued to delude themselves that there was something mysterious and enigmatic about Stalin's intentions. Senator Vandenburg described the Soviet foreign policy as "the supreme conundrum of our times." And I was amazed to see in the *New York Times* magazine only two weeks ago the statement that Stalin differs from Hitler in that Hitler frankly wrote down and published his plans and Stalin did not.

Stalin's plans were written down and published long before Hitler's, and only a man who can't read has any excuse for not knowing what they are. They are published in books signed by him, currently revised by him, and translated by his authorization into all civilized languages, selling in millions of copies and adhered to as a textbook and campaign book by his followers in every corner of the globe. . . .

Here, in one sentence from Stalin's book, *Problems of Leninism,* is the immutable bedrock of Soviet foreign policy:

"It is inconceivable that the Soviet Republic should continue to exist for a long period side by side with imperialist states—ultimately one or the other must conquer."

Imperialist states means us. And this, mind you, is not something Stalin said in the 1920's, or before the war, or after the war, or last week, or yesterday. It is what he is saying right now in thirty languages to hundreds of millions of people. The book containing this notification of our doom is being shipped about our country in an excellent English translation that sells for twenty-five cents a copy. Has Secretary Marshall read it? Has President Truman or Governor Dewey read it? I see no sign in their speeches that they ever even heard of it.

"What is the Soviet Union," Stalin continues, "what is our country as it builds socialism, but a base for the world revolution?"

And, does anybody ask whether such a revolution can be accomplished without violence and without dictatorship? "Obviously not." (I am still quoting.)

And, what is dictatorship? "The scientific concept, dictatorship, means nothing more or less than power which rests on violence which is not limited by any laws . . . Dictatorship means power resting on violence, not on law."

That, in words quoted as gospel from Lenin, is Stalin's blueprint for the future of our country. That, from his own lips, is his foreign policy.

And he doesn't want any confusion about it among his American disciples. He doesn't want them to take seriously the hocus-pocus about peace and democracy with which he pulls the wool over the eyes of our leaders. So he had his deputy, Andrei Vishinsky, as soon as the war ended, make a speech in which he recalled these explicit texts of Lenin and gave notice that they are still in force. And, at the risk of all America reading it—even, by some prodigious accident, our great diplomats—he had the speech translated into English and published in the bulletin of the Soviet Embassy in Washington.

Just let me read you a sentence from that bulletin, dated November 17, 1945:

"Lenin exposed the sweet-sounding nonsense about a calm and smooth development of bourgeois society into socialism —nonsense to the effect that it is not in the fires of battle, not by means of revolutionary struggle, but in reconciling and smoothing out class contradictions that the socialist transformation of the state is to be effected.

"Lenin developed the teachings of Marx in the important question of smashing the bourgeois state apparatus."

Now, anybody who ever looked into the writings of Lenin, and followed their application by Stalin, knows what that phrase means, "smash the bourgeois state apparatus." It means in the United States seize the public buildings and purge them of every official and every clerk, and every clerk's assistant who is loyal to the ideals, or imbued with the habits of free enterprise and representative government; go into the buildings and clean them out at the point of a bayonet, disinfect them of democracy by summary executions and prison camps, and establish a ruthless one-party dictatorship in this country which will take over and run our commerce, our industry, our labor unions, our every last little sewing circle and society for the conservation of bird life. That's what it means.

Well, I rather insolently accused this government of ignorance, and I want to give you a concrete example.

I have shown you in his own words what Stalin's plan for the United States is. Now, I want to read you the attitude which Secretary Marshall takes to that blueprint of our future. He was appearing before the House Committee on Foreign Affairs last spring to oppose a proposal to revise the charter of the United Nations in such a way as to make the Soviet Union either fish or cut bait, either come in on a movement to protect world peace or get out—a very sensible and practical proposal which was endorsed by a large number of senators as well as representatives. Secretary Marshall opposed. He said:

"Since the adoption of the charter in 1945 it has become progressively clearer that serious misconceptions prevail in the minds of the leaders of the Soviet Union concerning Western civilization. It is a misconception to suppose that differing systems cannot live side by side in peace under the basic rules prescribed by the charter of the United Nations. These rules are obligatory upon all members. A fundamental task of our foreign policy is to dispel the misconceptions of the Soviet leaders."

"It has become progressively clearer . . ."

Was there anything unclear in those sentences I read to you from Stalin's book, the Bible of the communist revolution? Did those things I read to you sound like misconceptions? They are not misconceptions, and they are not conceptions, either. They are fixed, fanatical, deeply grounded, hundred-year-old passionate purposes—purposes to destroy our world and build a different one in its place. And I think it is plainly obvious that Secretary Marshall never read the book, or any of the books, the whole library of books, in which this purpose has been discussed back and forth for a hundred years.

I have the highest esteem for General Marshall as a soldier, a man who played a major part in defeating one totalitarian state at war. As a Secretary of State, a foreign minister engaged in trying to defeat another at peace, he simply doesn't pass the examination at all. He gets a low "D" for having neglected his homework, for trying to get by as Secretary of State of the United States without studying. That's why I say that ignorance at Washington is the basic cause of our trouble.

Stalin regards this situation, which we call peace, or an attempt to make peace, as a truce between the Soviet Union and her enemies. He always calls them "our enemies"—the Western democracies. He will employ that truce to jockey for every position, both in our country and outside of it, which will enable him or his followers, or their successors, when the hour strikes, to seize the power in this country, overthrow our government, and establish a one-party dictatorship. And in this process he will be withheld by no principles of honor or morality whatever.

Stalin has often boasted himself an obedient pupil of his

master, Lenin. Lenin advocated trickery and lies and smear campaigns, and absolute immorality as a method of politics, just as explicitly as Hitler ever did. "Communist morality," he said, "is identical with the fight to strengthen the dictatorship of the proletariat." He made that statement to an all-union congress of communist youth. That was what he had to say about morality to the children of Russia. Think of it! And Stalin was brought up almost from boyhood in this doctrine.

From the days when he robbed banks and bombed bank agents in order to replenish the treasury of the Bolshevik party to this present time when he seizes capitalist nations under the pretense of anxiety for security or distrust of the warmongers, he has been guided absolutely by Lenin's principle of the subordination of moral principle to the principle of expediency in the grab for power.

Stalin's chief trickery and deceit at the present moment is to pretend that it is America and not the Soviet Union which is trying to conquer and dominate Europe and the world, to pretend that he distrusts our motives, including the Marshall Plan or the Truman policy. The only thing Stalin distrusts about America is the miracle of our gullibility. He doubts whether we will continue forever to misunderstand his purposes or imagine that there is something enigmatic about his foreign policy. He is afraid that some day we will turn the page from his public pronouncements about peace and democracy to his private instructions to his own followers as a totalitarian Marxist, to the people upon whom he depends to carry out his aims. He is afraid that in that process some day we will just turn the page and read in his own words, quoted from his master, Lenin, this basic statement:

"It is inconceivable that the Soviet Republic should continue to exist for a long period side by side with imperialist states—ultimately one or the other must conquer."

Or, in words whose rhythm is more familiar to our ears: "Civilization cannot long survive half totalitarian and half free."

That statement should be the basis of our foreign policy as it is of Stalin's. We must repeat to ourselves with all force and solemnity, until there isn't a flicker of self-deception left, until there isn't any least intention to creep under or creep out of the truth of it—we must repeat this statement: "There will be no peace on earth as long as the Communist regime survives in Moscow."

That's the third fact which I call upon you to confront today. I think it flows with unanswerable logic from the other two. So long as the Russian people and the people of the satellite nations are held in the grip of this totalitarian one-party tyranny and drilled in the impassioned dogmas of the Marxist-Leninist-Stalinist doctrine of world domination we will never get out of the nightmare in which we live. Until an American statesman comes along who has the grit, and the fighting pluck and the pride of power to see this fact and base his foreign policy on it, neither peace nor democracy will ever get a firm foothold on this earth.

This doesn't mean that war is inevitable between the United States and the Soviet Union. War is inevitable if we continue the policy of self-deception, if in the foolish attempt to make one world out of two we let Stalin drive us back and back until we have to fight a war of national survival. We saw that happen in the case of Hitler and we paid the cost. Let's not make that mistake again.

We must be well and fully armed. We must learn to think of international problems as the Marxists do—in the terms of material force, not Christian persuasion. We must indeed prepare for war. But that we are doing. What we are not doing is using the instruments of peace in order to stop the Soviet expansion and bring on the day when this tyrannical regime will be overthrown either by a patriotic putsch or a popular revolution.

That is what we must do. The chief instrument of course is the United Nations. Stalin is using the United Nations as an instrument to destroy itself, a sounding board to rally the masses for the totalitarian world revolution. We must use it as an instrument of democracy, a sounding board to rally the masses of the satellite nations who hate their oppressor, and the Russian people. And we must use other and unorthodox methods. We must use all the methods to promote a democratic world revolution that Stalin uses to promote a totalitarian world revolution, except those which involve deceit and distrust, a manipulation instead of an enlightenment of the people. And we must never forget and never let the world forget that our allies in this undertaking are the oppressed people, or more particularly the opposition, the silent or exiled opposition parties and leaders of the people in the countries oppressed by the tyrant, not excepting Russia itself.

Either we will adopt this astute and informed diplomatic offensive or we will be backed into a belated and blundering defensive war. I can see no other alternative except to surrender our free, rational, kindly and democratic way of life, surrender civilization itself, and bow down to the gangster-god.

RECOMMENDED FOR FURTHER READING

The Road to Serfdom by F. A. Hayek
Socialism by Ludwig von Mises
The Social Crisis of Our Time by Wilhelm Roepke
Capitalism and the Historians by F. A. Hayek, T. S. Ashton,
    Louis M. Hacker, Bertrand de Jouvenel, W. H. Hutt
Economics in One Lesson by Henry Hazlitt
Collectivism, A False Utopia by William Henry Chamberlin
Assignment in Utopia by Eugene Lyons
Lost Illusion by Freda Utley
Stalin by Boris Souvarine
Witness by Whittaker Chambers
Verdict of Three Decades by Julien Steinberg
Essays on Freedom and Power by Lord Acton
The Machiavellians by James Burnham
The Ruling Class by Gaetano Mosca
Political Parties by Robert Michels
The Socialist Tragedy by Ivor Thomas
The Open Society and Its Enemies by Karl Raimund Popper
The Servile State by Hilaire Belloc